World Food
ITALY

MARKS &
SPENCER

LINDA DOESER

World Food
ITALY

Marks and Spencer p.l.c.

Baker Street, London, W1U 8EP

www.marksandspencer.com

Copyright © Exclusive Editions 2003

Created and produced by The Bridgewater Book Company Ltd.

Project Editor Nicola Wright

Project Designer Michael Whitehead

Photography Simon Punter

Home Economists Ricky Turner and Clare Nolan

Additional photography Max Alexander, Terry Jeavons and Alistair Plumb

Front cover photography Mike Hemsley at Walter Gardiner

ISBN: 1-84273-913-1

Printed in China

NOTES FOR THE READER

• This book uses both metric and imperial measurements. Follow the same
units of measurement throughout; do not mix metric and imperial.

• All spoon measurements are level: teaspoons are assumed to be 5 ml, and
tablespoons are assumed to be 15 ml.

• Unless otherwise stated, milk is assumed to be full fat, eggs and individual
vegetables such as potatoes are medium, and pepper is freshly ground
black pepper.

• Recipes using raw or very lightly cooked eggs should be avoided by infants,
the elderly, pregnant women, convalescents, and anyone suffering from
an illness.

• The times given are an approximate guide only. Preparation times differ
according to the techniques used by different people and the cooking times
may also vary from those given.

contents

INTRODUCTION

10 It has often been said, with some justification, that the essence of Italian cooking can be summed up in two words: seasonal and regional. There is another, perhaps less precise factor that lies at the heart of this wonderful cuisine – the legendary Italian love of good things, including good food. Learning the skills of cooking starts at an early age, as recipes and techniques are handed down the generations, and so too does an appreciation of well-prepared meals, whether a plate of *al dente* pasta topped with a simple sauce of freshly picked, sun-ripened tomatoes, a slow-cooked, aromatic beef stew or a perfect seafood risotto.

Italians are natural gourmets, almost from the day they are born, and this, combined with their sheer enthusiasm and exuberance, makes eating in Italy a magical experience. Italians truly appreciate their food and little gives them greater pleasure than sharing it with friends and family. They perceive the rich harvests of the land and sea, rivers and lakes as gifts to be used and enjoyed to the full. No Tuscan would ever consider a low-fat alternative to what is probably the best olive oil produced anywhere, no Neapolitan will count the calories in a plate of pasta and, although Roman women are among the most elegant and sophisticated in the world, they will tackle a dish of *saltimbocca* with genuine relish and a hearty appetite.

Of course, it is an additional advantage that the Italian diet, like that of most Mediterranean countries, is one of the healthiest today. Vegetables and fruit play a leading role, while complex carbohydrates in the form of pasta, rice, polenta and bread are integral to informal and formal meals. Olive oil, one of the staples of Italy's cuisine, is high in mono-unsaturated fat, which is thought to help lower blood cholesterol levels. Variety – both within the range of courses in a single meal and among the dishes served from season to season – is the key and also the classic route to a healthy diet. The occasional indulgence in cream, butter, Parmesan cheese, red meat or any other of those ingredients that throw food faddists and health freaks into paroxysms of self-denial, is simply a way of life for Italians and part of a natural balance.

cooking through the year

Italians respect their ingredients and insist on the best quality, so although modern transportation and refrigeration mean that they can buy artichokes or peaches all year round, they still prefer to use seasonal produce that, if possible, is locally grown. They remain firmly in touch with that special, now sometimes forgotten pleasure of tasting the new crop: tender young peas of early summer, luscious grapes in autumn, or the crisp bite of winter's fennel.

In provincial towns and villages, people shop daily for fresh produce in the markets and plan the day's menu around what looks, feels and smells to be in peak condition. In major cities, fruit, vegetables and fish are rarely bought much in advance, despite the pace and demands of city dwelling. Even when the season is right, if the particular specimens on sale are not of the highest quality or have yet to reach perfection, they are left on the stall and a different dish will be prepared for lunch or dinner. A shopping list is only the starting point and numerous deviations from the original plan are a welcome delight. It is probably true to say that for Italians the choice of vegetables is the most crucial part of menu planning.

This emphasis on seasonal, locally sourced produce and uncompromising quality has had a lasting effect on the style of Italian cuisine. Simplicity is the essence, so that the flavour of ingredients is never masked by elaborate sauces, haphazard combinations or flamboyant garnishes. Fish, for example, is frequently sprinkled with a few herbs and chargrilled before being served with just a splash of olive oil and a wedge of lemon to squeeze over it – but the fish is freshly caught, the herbs are straight from the garden, the olive oil is flavoursome and aromatic and the lemon has recently been picked while still warm from ripening in the sun. The lunchtime spaghetti may be served with no more than a plain tomato sauce – but the pasta dough was mixed and kneaded earlier in the morning, the tomatoes are only hours off the vine and the whole dish is sprinkled with freshly grated Parmesan, produced by a jealously guarded, centuries-old tradition of cheesemaking.

regional diversity

Italy has only been a unified country, first a kingdom and then a republic, for under 150 years. Until the mid-19th century, it consisted of independent regions and city states and in many ways these have never really disappeared. Italians have a saying that there is

no such thing as an Italian and prefer to think of themselves as Romans, Venetians, Tuscans, Neapolitans, Florentines and so on. Each region inspires fierce patriotism in its sons and daughters, who take great pride in their local customs, architecture, history, scenery, traditions and cuisine. Indeed, this local loyalty extends to individual towns and villages within the same region – a devotion known as *campanilismo* that sparks considerable rivalry.

One result of this powerful local allegiance is that Italian cooking remains more regional than anywhere else in Europe. The distinctive culinary styles are further emphasized by the engrained habit of buying locally grown produce. Not that this means that the

Gondolas on the Grand Canal in Venice

despite the trade in ideas, Italian cooking remains firmly fixed in its distinctive regional roots

country's cuisine is locked in the past. Indeed, new dishes and variations of traditional recipes are continually developed, especially in cosmopolitan, sophisticated cities, such as Rome, Milan, Venice and Bologna. Nevertheless, Italians have enormous respect for and a great love of their culinary traditions.

The most obvious culinary divide is between the north and south of the country and this exists partly as a result of geography and partly through historical and cultural inheritance. Dairy farming in the cooler, wetter north produces butter, cream and cheese, which feature in the cooking in this part of Italy. Similarly, both rice and maize are widely cultivated, so risotto and polenta are staples in Piedmont, Lombardy, the Veneto and Liguria. The south of Italy, on the other hand, is the home of pasta, olives and olive oil, tomatoes, aubergines and citrus fruits. At one time, this invisible culinary border was impenetrable, until the enterprising Tuscans began to open restaurants in the south and introduced their own specialities, using steak (*bistecca*), bean dishes and their magnificent Chianti Classico. Other regions quickly followed and the north, in turn, learned of *mozzarella di bufala* and goat's milk cheeses, pizza and Marsala, the potent, fortified wine from Sicily.

However, despite the trade in ideas, Italian cooking remains firmly fixed in its distinctive regional roots. Of course, this does not mean that you will not find spaghetti in Milan or cured ham in Calabria, but

The Piazza del Campo in Sienna is a popular place for cafés and restaurants. Visitors can sit outdoors and enjoy good food and sunshine

To travel through Italy is to take a voyage of culinary exploration ... each province has its own distinctive cooking style and repertoire of dishes

Italians are far more reluctant to relinquish their traditional, regional dishes than most other Europeans.

the regions

To travel through Italy is to take a voyage of culinary exploration. The north–south culinary divide is only part of the story, for each province has its own distinctive cooking style and repertoire of dishes – and, naturally, each considers itself the best.

In the most northerly provinces, the influence of Austria and the southern Tyrol is immediately apparent in the rich soups and substantial dumplings on offer, especially in Alto Adige. Rivers and lakes in Trentino are an abundant source of fresh fish, and game is plentiful in the mountains. Simple meat, offal and pasta dishes are prepared throughout the region and hearty pot-roasts are a speciality of Alto Adige.

In the northwest is Piedmont, at the foot of the Alps, yet it feels more like a mountain enclave itself. Its foggy autumns are a time of pilgrimage for wealthy gastronomes from around the world to savour its wonderful white truffles. Their delicate aroma can perfume an entire room and they are seldom more delicious than when grated raw over pasta or risotto. They are also traditionally cooked in a pasta sauce with butter, garlic, cream and anchovies. Game, such as hare, is abundant and comforting meat stews and casseroles, almost always with polenta, are served during the cold winters. Beef in Barolo, one of Piedmont's best red wines, is a classic dish that can stand comparison with *boeuf*

bourguignon and, indeed, the region has strong links with neighbouring France. This is also Italy's largest rice-growing region. Piedmont is known for *bagna cauda*, a hot, garlic and anchovy sauce for dipping vegetables. The region's main city, Turin, is renowned for its sweetmeats, cakes and desserts, many of them based on the local hazelnuts. Piedmont's smallest Alpine neighbour, the Valle d'Aosta, is the home of Fontina, a delicious melting cheese, which is often served in a similar way to a Swiss fondue.

Friuli in the northeast and the Veneto, the region around Venice, are famous for magnificent seafood and fabulous risottos. The deceptively simple *Risi e Bisi* (see page 102) is a Venetian speciality that opened the Doge's annual St Mark's banquet. So too is a melt-in-the-mouth dish of calf's liver *in agrodol*ce, a sweet-and-sour sauce made from wine and balsamic vinegars. Polenta is a staple here, usually served as an accompaniment to meat and fish dishes, but pasta is far less common. San Daniele in Friuli produces a cured ham that some consider to be even finer than the better-known prosciutto from Parma, and cotechino sausage is as much as speciality of the Veneto as it is of neighbouring Emilia-Romagna. The region is not renowned for sweet dishes, but does specialize in unique, delicately flavoured lemon biscuits called *bacioli*.

Lombardy lies in the centre of the northern regions and its culinary influences are equally mixed – French, Austrian, even Spanish, and Venetian. Its dairy produce is second to none, so butter is used in preference to olive oil, and pasta is invariably topped with a creamy sauce. However, it is in cheesemaking that Lombardy excels – taleggio, stracchino, mascarpone, ribiola, Grana Padano and, one of the

Bernini's Colonnade, built for Pope Alexander VII, in Rome

Overleaf Sunset over Florence. *In the city, fresh, well-cooked food can always be enjoyed with a bottle of Chianti*

great cheeses, Gorgonzola, are all produced here. Like the Veneto, Lombardy claims to have invented risotto and, certainly, *Risotto alla Milanese* (see page 98) is a world-famous dish. It is invariably served with that other classic from Milan, *osso bucco*, succulent veal shanks braised in wine and garnished with *gremolata*, a piquant mix of parsley, lemon rind and garlic. Beef and veal are the most popular meats in this region and it produces an air-cured beef equivalent of prosciutto, called *bresaola*. Pork is only slightly less common here and pancetta, sausages and salami all feature in Lombardy specialities. Sweet recipes include panettone, a Christmas bread from Milan, as well as tiramisù, based on local mascarpone cheese.

The coast of Liguria is renowned for its rich diversity of fish and seafood, while the interior of the region produces tasty seasoned, stuffed dishes. The ancient port of Genoa was a gateway for the spice trade and this is reflected in Liguria's culinary heritage. However, Genoa is probably best known as the home of pesto, a mix of fresh basil, garlic, pine nuts, olive oil and Parmesan cheese. The Genoese believe that they grow the best basil in the world and are said to take a locally grown supply of the herb with them when they travel. Basil and other fresh herbs are widely used in Ligurian cooking, and flavour the local pasta dough.

Focaccia, that dimpled flat bread, is very popular in Liguria, served as an accompaniment or made into sandwiches. It is traditionally baked in a wood oven, plain or flavoured with ham, cheese, olives, sun-dried tomatoes, onions or herbs. Italian bakeries produce very large loaves, weighing several kilos and sell it cut into more manageable pieces. Almost as popular in Liguria are gnocchi, small, melt-in-the-mouth dumplings that are poached in lightly salted boiling water and served drizzled with olive oil, tossed in

The Tower of Pisa, in Tuscany

grated Parmesan or in a creamy sauce. The tradition here, as in northern Italy as a whole, is to make them from mashed potatoes combined with a little flour, but gnocchi can also be made from semolina.

Emilia-Romagna, two rather different provinces united into a single administrative territory, is a gourmet's paradise. Not only does the architecture of its principal city, Bologna, date back to the Middle Ages, so too does its reputation as a gastronomic centre. The region itself is an agricultural cornucopia – wheat, tomatoes, rice, maize, fruit and vegetables are grown on the rich soils of the Po Valley, while cattle graze the grasslands and pigs are raised throughout the countryside. Emilia-Romagna is world famous for three products in particular: Parma ham, Parmesan cheese and balsamic vinegar, and it can also offer an extensive range of other specialities: cured meats, such as mortadella, salami, and stuffed pasta. The trademark dish of Bologna must be *Tagliatelle alla Bolognese* (see page 70), with *fritto misto* a close second. *Bollito Misto* (see page 122) is a speciality of Modena, home of the best balsamic vinegar, as is *zampone* (stuffed pig's trotter), while the entire region boasts a wide choice of dishes made with beef, chicken, ham and game, as well as magnificent fish and seafood.

There is a difference – historical and culinary – between Emilia and Romagna. Emilia has aristocratic, even royal connections. Parma was closely associated with Napoleon's second wife and her chefs were responsible for the legacy of fine pastries in the region. Savoury dishes are rich and subtle, sparing neither cream nor butter. Romagna, on the other hand, has a more peasant heritage and the dishes from this part of the region are robust and flavoured generously with herbs, onion and garlic. The Romagnols also favour olive oil, rather than butter.

In central Italy, landlocked Umbria has no pretensions to gastronomy, but the superb quality

Emilia-Romagna is world famous for ... Parma ham, Parmesan cheese and balsamic vinegar

of the ingredients, whether freshwater fish, pork, lamb or game, amply justifies a simple approach to preparation and cooking. The local olive oil has a distinctive if subtle flavour and it is put to good use in cooking and dressing dishes before serving. Black truffles grow in this cooler highland region and feature in local dishes during late autumn and winter, when they are in season.

The neighbouring Marches region on the Adriatic coast boasts a rather more sophisticated style of cooking than Umbria and is rightly famous for the quality of its charcuterie, especially cured pork and sausages. Pork is the most popular meat in the region, although game, especially wood pigeon, classically served with lentils, is a local speciality.

Tuscany has become one of Europe's prime holiday destinations, not only because of the clear blue skies, golden sunshine, rolling green hills and charming, half-concealed, sun-baked villages, but also its truly marvellous food. Olive trees were first introduced to Tuscany by the ancient Greeks and today the region produces what many claim to be the best olive oil in the world. The keynote of Tuscan cooking is simplicity – a few, absolutely perfect ingredients are combined to emphasize rather than disguise the flavours.

Vegetables grow abundantly in Tuscany's warm climate and well-drained soil and beans are almost synonymous with its cuisine. Indeed, neighbouring regions have nicknamed Tuscans *i mangia fagioli* – the bean-eaters. *Ribollita*, a cabbage and bean soup thick enough to be called a stew, is probably Tuscany's most famous dish, but the region is also well known for the quality of its beef, pork, chicken

the red wine of Tuscany, Chianti Classico, enjoys a world-wide reputation to match its olive oil

and wild boar. Fresh herbs play an essential role. *Pan scicco*, a dense loaf made from only flour, yeast and water, is unique to the region and is often used to make bruschetta. Pecorino cheese originated in the area around the city of Sienna, which is also the home of the popular Christmas cake *Panforte* (see page 242). Florence is credited with the invention of the melt-in-the-mouth dessert *Zabaglione* (see page 239) and the red wine of Tuscany, Chianti Classico, enjoys a world-wide reputation to match its olive oil.

Inevitably, the best of the regional cuisines gravitates towards Rome, capital of Italy and of the province of Lazio. Roman restaurants are among the best in Europe but, perhaps because of their clientele's sophisticated taste, the food preparation tends towards elegant simplicity. Even so, rich sauces and robust flavours abound throughout the region. Pasta and semolina gnocchi (here oven-baked rather than poached) are more popular than rice, and the local meat – lamb and veal in particular – is excellent. Rome's signature dish could be said to be *Saltimbocca alla Romana* (see page 146), a subtly simple recipe for pan-fried veal escalopes flavoured with sage. Offal, especially stewed tripe, is also a speciality. Much of the food in Lazio is well seasoned and flavoured with a wide variety of herbs.

Abruzzi and Molise are almost invariably bracketed together, although they no longer form a single administrative region. The food in these mountainous areas is very traditional and rural, based on locally produced cured meats, sausages and cheeses. Lamb is the most popular meat, while the coastal areas feature an abundance of fish and seafood.

Although not unique to Abruzzi, the exceptionally hot peperoncino chilli is widely grown here, known to the locals as *diavoletto*, little devil. A speciality of Lazio, west of Abruzzi, is *Pasta all'Arrabbiata* (see page 87), flavoured with these hot little devils. When the chillies have been harvested, they are plaited and hung outside the farmhouses to dry in summer to provide 'central heating' in winter dishes.

The Pugliese are known as *i mangia foglie*, the leaf-eaters, because of their legendary vegetable dishes. Puglia or Apulia, in the heel of Italy, also produces fruit, particularly figs and melons, olives, herbs and superb mushrooms. Pasta is immensely popular and some shapes are unique to the region. The favourite meat of Puglia is lamb, either spit-roasted or stewed with fresh herbs, but the local veal is also magnificent. The Adriatic fishing port of Brindisi is the place to eat memorable seafood risottos and other specialities made with octopus, oysters or mussels.

The Campania region marks another culinary frontier – that between fresh and dried pasta. The city of Naples first produced packaged dry pasta, rather than fresh egg pasta, back in the 15th century and the rest, as they say, is history. Naples has many other claims to fame, among them the invention of the pizza. Beginning life as a humble slice of bread dough, topped with tomato purée and cheese, then baked, this versatile snack has conquered the world and the choice of pizza toppings today is infinite.

Meat is a rarity in Campania, but its absence is more than adequately balanced by the abundance and variety of fish and seafood, especially sea bream, red mullet, squid, prawns and clams. Pasta with clams is an essentially Campanian combination and typically it is served in two forms – white sauce or tomato sauce – each with its own passionate devotees. Tomatoes are the quintessential Campanian vegetable

Lifestyles and traditions vary from region to region and from town to village

Visitors to a piazza enjoying a coffee-break

and appear in almost every course, especially as a colourful and tasty sauce for pasta. One of the region's rare meat dishes, *Bistecca alla Pizzaiola* (see page 127), is less famous for its beef than it is for the sauce of tomatoes, garlic and onions. The region also produces two major cheeses: mozzarella and provolone. Mozzarella is thought to have originated with the introduction of water buffalo from India in about AD 600, but history remains obstinately silent as to why these animals first appeared. Mozzarella, tomato and basil salad originated on the tiny island of Capri and on mainland Campania it is invariably called *insalata caprese*. Campanian desserts reflect a more sophisticated, cosmopolitan past and include

some superb pastries – among them lemon-filled profiteroles from Amalfi.

Sheep-farming is the main occupation in the mountainous region of Basilicata in the arch of the 'boot' of Italy, so sweet-flavoured, succulent lamb features in the local cuisine, but so too do pork and game. Many fine local cheeses are also produced. The cured meats and salami of the region are often spiced with home-grown peperoncino chillies, which tend to be milder than those from Abruzzi. Freshwater fish, including eels, are abundant in the many lakes. Fruit and vegetables flourish and robust soups keep out the winter chills. Pasta is a staple here.

Calabria is situated in the toe of Italy's boot and its climate is perfect for growing citrus fruits, olives and an immense variety of vegetables. Pasta is a staple and is usually served with a robust vegetable sauce that may include aubergines, baby artichokes or sweet peppers. Desserts are often based on locally grown almonds and sweetened with honey or include fresh fruit, particularly figs. Wild mushrooms proliferate and flavour stews, sauces and salads. Chicken and game, such as rabbit, are the main types of meat. Fish features on the menu, with swordfish and tuna being great favourites. Pizza is popular, often with a seafood topping.

Sicily, the island football to Italy's boot, offers a cuisine that is quite different from any on the mainland. This partly stems from the fertile, volcanically enriched soils on the slopes of Mount Etna and, even more, from the island's multi-national and multi-cultural heritage. Sicily has been an irresistible lure to invaders over the centuries – influenced by the Etruscans, Phoenicians, Carthaginians, Greeks, Romans, Arabs, Spanish, French and Austrians, as well as, of course, by mainland Italians. While Neapolitans will never concede defeat, there is a claim that pasta was introduced first to Sicily by the Arabs and spread from there to mainland Italy. Arabs also brought spices and sweet confectionery and encouraged the raising of sheep and goats. Fish plays a starring role in Sicilian cooking, notably tiny anchovies, sea bass, sardines, swordfish and tuna.

The island can be credited with being the first place to can tuna. Meat, whether lamb, kid, game or chicken, tends to be kept for high days and holidays, but vegetables are plentiful: spinach, aubergines, artichokes, pumpkin and other squashes, peppers, peas, broad beans, chickpeas and tomatoes are prepared in a variety of imaginative ways. *Caponata* (see page 54), aubergines in a sweet-and-sour sauce, is a Sicilian antipasto enjoyed far beyond the island's shores, while the local tomato paste is the most intensely concentrated of any made. Sicilian capers packed in salt are widely exported. Lemons are used in

both sweet and savoury dishes and oranges grow in abundance. Sicily produces the sweetest almonds in the world and these, together with the local thyme-flavoured honey, feature in both desserts and confectionery. Beautifully moulded marzipan fruits grace confectioners' windows like little works of art. Another Sicilian claim is the invention of ice cream – certainly their granitas, slushy water ices, are popular for cooling down in the island's hot summer. Other tempting sweet concoctions include *Crostata di Ricotta* (see page 232), *Cassata* (see page 248), doughnut-like *sfinci*, *zuppa inglese* (trifle), nougat and amaretti.

Italy's other main island, Sardinia, is different again. The Sardinians have kept themselves apart and their

Sicily has been an irresistible lure to invaders ... Etruscans, Phoenicians, Carthaginians, Greeks, Romans, Arabs, Spanish, French and Austrians as well as, of course ... mainland Italians

way of life, customs and cooking have remained very traditional. Surprisingly, fish and seafood do not play an especially popular role in the diet, although tuna, red mullet, sea bass, lobsters and mussels are abundant. However, game, including wild boar, and offal are important and pigs and sheep are reared all over the island. Spit-roasted suckling pig could be described as the 'national' dish, while roast lamb is invariably the choice for Easter Sunday. *Fregola*, tiny soup pasta shapes resembling couscous, are a speciality of Sardinia. Fruit grows well, despite the very dry summers. The island is smothered in *mirto*,

Mozzarella is perfect for melting, developing a stringy texture that seems to have been made for pizza toppings.

myrtle, which perfumes the air and is used in all kinds of cooking and to flavour the local liqueur. Typical southerners, the Sardinians produce mouthwatering confectionery, cakes and desserts, often sweetened with the local honey.

cheese

The ancient Greeks introduced the art of cheesemaking to Italy, the Romans improved the technique and over the centuries the Italians have mastered it. The different regions produce a range of hard, semi-soft, soft and fresh cheeses from cow's, ewe's, goat's and buffalo's milk.

The most famous of all Italian cheeses, Parmesan, is a hard cheese made from cow's milk that can be produced only in a zone around Parma that is tightly defined by law. Parmesan made within this registered area is stamped with the words Parmigiano Reggiano on the rind. The cheese is aged for a minimum of two years, sometimes much longer, to give it a crumbly texture and a pleasant, slightly salty flavour. Parmesan may be eaten on its own or with fresh fruit, but it is best known for grating over soups, pasta, polenta and vegetables. Though ready-grated Parmesan can be bought, it is better bought in a single piece and kept wrapped in foil in the fridge to be freshly grated as required.

A similar, but less good-quality cheese, Grana Padano, is also made in the Po Valley. It is grainier in texture and has a sharper, saltier flavour. It can be used in the same way as Parmesan.

Pecorino is the generic term for all ewe's milk cheeses. It is a hard cheese with a salty, pungent flavour. The best are said to come from Rome and Sardinia. Look out for *pecorino romano* and *pecorino sardo*. The former is usually matured for a period of about 18 months. This gives it a stronger, sharper flavour than cheeses that are matured for only a few weeks. Pecorino can be used in much the same way as Parmesan for sprinkling over robust dishes that can match its strength. Store, wrapped in foil, in the refrigerator for up to a month.

Fontina, from the Valle d'Aosta in the Italian Alps, is made from unpasteurized cow's milk. It is a semi-hard cheese, with a high fat content, a mild, nutty flavour and a creamy texture. It is delicious eaten on its own and excellent for cooking, as it melts well. It is the traditional choice for *fonduta*, the Italian equivalent of fondue.

Another high-fat, semi-hard cheese is taleggio, from Lombardy. It has a mild flavour with a salty tang. It melts well without becoming stringy, which makes it perfect for cooking, but it is equally delicious eaten on its own.

Gorgonzola can claim to be the king of Italy's blue cheeses, although its veining is more green than blue. It is a creamy cheese with a high fat content and the flavour can range from piquant to very strong, but it should never be offensive, nor its smell unpleasant. It originated in the village of Gorgonzola in Lombardy, where the cows rested on the long journey down from the mountains to their winter pastures. The village has long been subsumed by Milan and the cheese is now made all over the region. Gorgonzola is wonderful eaten on its own and it also excellent for cooking as the flavour mellows during heating. It is used in creamy pasta sauces, stirred into risottos or polenta or as a filling for pancakes.

Dolcelatte is a mild form of Gorgonzola. Torta is a layered cheese made from Gorgonzola and mascarpone, which is exceptionally rich with a phenomenal fat content.

*In the villas and farms of Italy, distinct regional traditions
of cheesemaking are proudly upheld*

Mascarpone is a delicately flavoured, fresh cream
cheese from Lombardy. Far too rich to eat on its own,
it is used like cream in both savoury and sweet dishes,
from pasta sauce to ice cream. It is best known in
desserts, particularly *Tiramisù* (see page 238).

Mozzarella may be even more widely used in Italian
cooking than Parmesan. It is a soft curd cheese, made
in layers, then shaped into balls and soaked in brine.
The balls are packed in whey to keep them fresh and
should be well drained before use. Mozzarella is
perfect for melting, developing a stringy texture that
seems to have been made for pizza toppings. Fresh

mozzarella is also delicious sliced and served with
tomatoes and basil (see *Insalata Tricolore* on page
220) or with sliced avocado in a salad. The best
mozzarella is made from buffalo's milk – *mozzarella
di bufala* – and is always worth buying in preference
to the more common cow's milk version as it has a
unique flavour. There is also a smoked mozzarella,
which is a lovely golden colour and something of an
acquired taste. Little balls of mozzarella are called
bocconcini, meaning little mouthfuls. Use fresh
mozzarella as soon after purchase as possible. If you
need to keep it, store it unopened in the fridge for no
more than 2 days.

Ricotta, meaning recooked, is made by reheating
the whey left over from the process of making hard

cheeses. It is a soft curd cheese with a relatively low fat content that may be made from cow's, ewe's or even goat's milk. It is widely used in both savoury and sweet dishes. It has a natural affinity with spinach and this combination is used to fill pasta and pancakes. *Crostata di ricotta* (Ricotta Cheesecake) is a delicious Sicilian speciality (see page 232). Use fresh ricotta on the day of purchase.

Ricotta salata is a hard, salted version of the cheese, made from the whey left over after making pecorino. It has a flaky texture and can be used like hard cheeses.

Provolone is a stretched curd cheese with a close, smooth texture. It is made with cow's or buffalo's milk and various different rennets. There are mild (*dolce*) and piquant (*piccante*) varieties, the latter made with kid's rennet. The best are from Campania and Puglia but it is made all over southern Italy, often with differing local names, and also in the Po Valley. It is used in pasta sauces and eaten on its own.

the italian meal

Whether you are dining in a noble *palazzo* or sharing supper in a farmhouse kitchen, all Italian meals take the same basic shape. The food may be more luxurious and the table more elegantly laid in one, but the care that has gone into the preparation and the enthusiasm with which the meal is eaten will be identical. The Italian love of food is legendary, matched only by a desire to share a meal with family and friends. Busy lives may have changed traditional social patterns, but it is a rare family that does not congregate around a huge table at least once a month for all the generations to eat, drink, talk and enjoy themselves.

Any Italian meal, lunch or dinner, centres on two savoury courses, which are of equal size and importance. These are known as the *primo* and *secondo*. In the evening the *primo* is usually soup, while at lunch it is more likely to be pasta, gnocchi or risotto, depending on the region. This is usually followed by a meat or fish dish, served with a single vegetable. Salad may be served with the *secondo* or afterwards. Dessert will generally be fresh fruit or perhaps cheese, unless the meal is a special one. On more formal occasions, an antipasto or appetizer may be served. This may be as simple as slices of salami and a bowl of olives or a more extensive selection of marinated vegetables or a terrine. Freshly baked bread is served with every meal and used, without restraint, for mopping up every last drop of the tasty sauces.

Freshly baked bread is served with every meal and used, without restraint, for mopping up every last drop of the tasty sauces

Wine and iced water are served with meals, although children may also have soft drinks. At the end of the meal, coffee, usually strong, black espresso, is drunk, perhaps with a liqueur, such as Amaretto, grappa, nocino or Strega, for the benefit of the digestion. If drinks are served before dinner, they might include an apéritif, such as Campari, vermouth or Punt e Mes, perhaps topped up with soda and ice.

The Italian approach to meal planning is to choose courses that are complementary, with harmonious flavours. A seafood soup, for example, would normally be followed by a fish *secondo*, such as *Filetti di Sogliole alla Pizzaiola* (see page 167). A robust pasta dish, on the other hand, might be followed by a full-flavoured stew, such as *Stufato alla Fiorentina* (see page 124), while a delicate risotto would probably precede chicken or veal, such as *Saltimbocca* (see page 146). Such careful menu planning takes time. Taking the trouble is natural enough when you are entertaining guests, but for many of us it can prove too much work for a midweek family supper. But you can still dine Italian style by making the *secondo* a lighter, vegetable dish, such as *Melanzane e Pomodori al Forno* (see page 197). Plus there are a great number of Italian dishes that are quick and easy to prepare, making perfect snacks, such as *Bruschetta* (see page 55).

Opposite Cetara is a charming fishing village on the Amalfi coast, famous for its alici *(similar to sardines) and tuna*

in the italian kitchen

Many, perhaps most, of the ingredients used by Italian cooks would have been familiar to our mothers and grandmothers: flour, butter – always unsalted in Italy, bacon, cream, potatoes, tomatoes and onions. Others have become familiar in the course of the past 20 or 30 years: aubergines, peppers, mozzarella, Parmesan, salami, pasta and even garlic. However, if you want to re-create the authentic flavour of Italy, do remember that it is not enough simply to follow the recipes; you must buy the freshest possible produce when it is in peak condition. Each section of this book introduces the important ingredients. First, though, a look at what to keep in stock.

store-cupboard items

Perfect fresh ingredients, from vegetables to herbs, lie at the heart of Italian cuisine, but store-cupboard items, such as olive oil and spices, are what give it true vitality. As with most items, you get what you pay for, so use the expensive ingredients wisely.

olive oil

Olive oil has a rich flavour because it is pressed directly from ripe fruit. There are a number of different qualities. Extra virgin olive oil is made from the first cold pressing – that is, without any other processing, such as heat treatment. The resulting oil is full of flavour with a very low acid content. It is the most expensive oil and the one to use for dressing salads or hot dishes, when flavour is paramount. Virgin olive oil comes from the second cold pressing and is only marginally more acidic. It is a wonderful all-purpose oil for cooking – apart from deep-frying. Oil that is simply labelled 'pure' is refined and may have been heat-treated. This oil is much less expensive and can be used for cooking, but is no good at all for dressings.

Many regions produce olive oil, and the flavours can vary considerably. The best is said to come from Lucca in Tuscany, but it is worth tasting different oils

Olive groves are a feature of many Italian landscapes

to find the one you like most. Olive oil from other countries, including Spain, Greece, France and, more recently, New Zealand, may be of excellent quality, but will not have that quintessentially Italian flavour.

Once opened, store olive oil in a cool dark place for no longer than 6 months.

vinegar

Given that Italy is the world's largest wine producer, it is not surprising that red and white wine vinegars are of very high quality. Always look for vinegar that has been fermented in oak casks, to ensure no trace of bitterness.

Balsamic vinegar is made in the area around Modena in Emilia-Romagna and is produced and matured – often for over 20 years – with the same loving care as wine. It has a uniquely mellow, rich, sweet flavour. It is very expensive, but because it is so distinctive only a little is required to lift dressings, marinades and sauces.

dried mushrooms

Porcini, also known as ceps, are the king of mushrooms. While they are at their most delicious when fresh, using dried porcini is an easy way to give an intense and aromatic mushroom flavour to sauces, stews and casseroles, and to enliven cultivated mushrooms. Porcini are available from supermarkets and delicatessens, and they are expensive, but a little goes a long way. Don't be tempted to buy cheap packets, which may contain other, inferior mushrooms. All dried mushrooms must be rehydrated before use; remember to use the soaking liquid in your cooking.

truffles

Fresh truffles are an extravagance that is probably beyond most family budgets. Canned truffles are available, but the whole ones are still very expensive. Truffle pieces and peelings are more modestly priced and can add a special flavour to many dishes. A few drops of truffle oil are the most economical way to add a wonderful aroma to pasta sauces, risottos and salads.

capers

These are the immature buds of a Mediterranean shrub, and are usually pickled in white wine vinegar or preserved in brine. Capers make a good addition to salads, crostini and pizza toppings. Sicilian capers are packed in salt, which enhances their flavour. They should be rinsed and dried before use. Caper berries are the fruit of the same shrub. They are larger than capers and have long stalks. Serve them with pre-dinner drinks or in salads.

dried chillies

Peperoncino chillies are added to many southern dishes. Italian delicatessens stock hot, Italian dried chillies, but other varieties or chilli flakes may be used if you can't take the heat.

saffron

The most expensive spice in the world comes from the dried stigmas of a type of crocus. In Italy, it is used to colour and flavour dishes, from *Risotto alla Milanese* to fish and seafood sauces. The threads are crumbled into the cooking liquid or soaked in a little stock or water then added to the dish with the soaking liquid. Saffron powder is available, but may be adulterated with the less pungent safflower.

fennel seeds

This sweet, liquorice-flavoured spice is a popular flavouring for seafood stews and is sprinkled on grilled fish. The seeds are often scattered over bread dough before baking and feature in the Florentine *finocchiona* salami.

SOUPS &
ANTIPASTI

Italian cooks may value tradition, but this does not prevent them from being wonderfully creative. Not only does virtually every region boast its own version of such familiar favourites as minestrone and bruschetta, so does almost every family. The soups and appetizers here are authentically Italian, but they are not and cannot be definitive, so feel free to experiment.

In Italy, soup is usually served as the *primo* at dinner and is regarded as being equally as important as the meat or fish *secondo* that follows, not merely a preliminary to the star attraction. Consequently, traditional Italian soups are not simply packed with flavour, but are often quite substantial. Vegetables predominate, whether beans in Tuscany, greens in Puglia or tomatoes in Campania. The best-known Italian vegetable soup has to be minestrone – *minestra* simply means soup. There are probably as many versions of the recipe as there are cooks in the country and it can be prepared with whatever vegetables are in season, providing no single flavour dominates and the combination is in balance. Depending on the region, tiny soup pasta or rice is added towards the end of the cooking time and, in the case of the Genoese version, pesto is stirred in to serve. Meat features far less frequently in Italian soups, except in the case of clear broths, when a good-quality beef consommé forms the basis. Fish and seafood, on the other hand, are used in profusion in lavish, colourful soups that are often so filling that they could more properly be called stews. It is always worth making Italian soups in large quantities, as many improve with keeping and virtually all of them freeze well. Add any rice or pasta when reheating.

Served before the meal, antipasti provide a wonderful opportunity for creativity. They are always tasty, light, appetizing and visually appealing, mainly based on cured meats, vegetables, seafood and salads.

Antipasti are often cold dishes and may be as simple as a platter of salami, served with olives and, perhaps, fresh fruit, such as melon or figs. Italy's superb cured ham, prosciutto, is also classically served with fruit, but pairs well with strongly flavoured salad vegetables, such as rocket, while nothing could be simpler or more impressive than *Carpaccio* (see page 46), thinly sliced fillet of beef marinated in lemon juice and extra virgin olive oil. Marinated vegetables, such as peppers, mushrooms and olives, are a popular antipasto, as their flavours are complementary and they look so tempting. Stuffed vegetables, usually served lukewarm or at room temperature to bring out

*In many regions and towns of Italy, cooks have
developed their own variations of traditional recipes*

*Overleaf In the heart of the agricultural region of Tuscany
lie olive groves and vineyards. Wheat is cultivated and
vegetables grow in abundance in the warm climate*

their full flavour, are another good choice. The range
is varied, including not just the obvious cup-shaped
peppers and tomatoes, but also aubergines, which are
a Ligurian speciality, and artichokes, which make up
a classic Roman dish.

Italians are said to eat more bread than any other
nation, so it is hardly surprising that tasty toasted
canapés are favourites for antipasti. The simplest is
fettunta, the name for toasted bread rubbed with
garlic, drizzled with olive oil and sprinkled with sea
salt. With a topping of cheese, tomatoes, olives,
anchovies or pesto, *fettunta* becomes *bruschetta*.
Crostini are similar and may be made with a bread or

a polenta base. Mozzarella cheese is a natural
companion for toast, as it melts so appealingly.
A delicious Roman antipasto consists of stacks of
small toast squares, sliced mozzarella, sliced tomato
and fresh basil leaves held together with skewers,
drizzled with olive oil and then baked for about
10 minutes in a very hot oven. Naples offers
Mozzarella in Carrozza (see page 58) – literally
mozzarella in carriages. In this recipe, cheese and
salami sandwiches are coated in an egg mixture and
deep-fried until golden. They are served with a
tomato, onion and garlic sauce – a dish substantial
enough to make a summer lunch.

*fettunta, the name for toasted bread
rubbed with garlic, drizzled with olive
oil and sprinkled with sea salt*

genoese vegetable soup
minestrone alla genovese

This classic vegetable soup is served with an equally classic pesto sauce that originated in the Ligurian port of Genoa. It makes a wonderful first course – primo – for an informal dinner with family and friends.

SERVES 8

2 onions, sliced

2 carrots, diced

2 celery sticks, sliced

2 potatoes, diced

115 g/4 oz French beans, cut into 2.5-cm/1-inch lengths

115 g/4 oz peas, thawed if using frozen

200 g/7 oz fresh spinach leaves, coarse stalk
   removed, shredded

2 courgettes, diced

225 g/8 oz Italian plum tomatoes, peeled*, deseeded
   and diced

3 garlic cloves, sliced thinly

4 tbsp extra virgin olive oil

2 litres/3½ pints vegetable or chicken stock

salt and pepper

140 g/5 oz dried stellete or other soup pasta

freshly grated Parmesan cheese, to serve

for the pesto

55 g/2 oz fresh basil leaves

15 g/½ oz pine kernels

1 garlic clove

salt

25 g/1 oz freshly grated Parmesan cheese

3 tbsp extra virgin olive oil

1 Put the onions, carrots, celery, potatoes, beans, peas, spinach, courgettes, tomatoes and garlic in a large, heavy-based saucepan, pour in the olive oil and stock and bring to the boil over a medium-low heat. Lower the heat and simmer gently for about 1½ hours.

2 Meanwhile, make the pesto. Put the basil, pine kernels, garlic and a pinch of salt into a mortar and pound to a paste with a pestle. Transfer to a bowl and gradually work in the Parmesan with a wooden spoon, followed by the olive oil to make a thick, creamy sauce. Cover with clingfilm and set aside in the refrigerator until required.

3 Season the soup to taste with salt and pepper and add the pasta. Cook for a further 8–10 minutes, until the pasta is tender, but still firm to the bite. The soup should be very thick. Stir in half the pesto, remove the saucepan from the heat and set aside to rest for 4 minutes. Taste and adjust the seasoning, adding more salt, pepper and pesto if necessary. (Any leftover pesto may be stored in a screw-top jar in the fridge for up to 2 weeks.) Ladle into warmed bowls and serve immediately. Hand round the freshly grated Parmesan cheese separately.

*cook's tip

To peel tomatoes, cut a cross in the base of each and place in a bowl. Cover with boiling water and leave for 30–45 seconds. Drain and plunge into cold water, then the skins will slide off easily.

fresh tomato soup
zuppa di pomodori

SERVES 4

1 tbsp olive oil

650 g/1 lb 7 oz plum tomatoes

1 onion, cut into quarters

1 garlic clove, sliced thinly

1 celery stick, chopped coarsely

500 ml/18 fl oz chicken stock

55 g/2 oz dried anellini or other soup pasta

salt and pepper

fresh flat-leaved parsley, chopped, to garnish

Make this refreshing soup in midsummer when sun-ripened tomatoes have maximum sweetness and flavour.

1 Pour the olive oil into a large, heavy-based saucepan and add the tomatoes, onion, garlic and celery. Cover and cook over a low heat for 45 minutes, occasionally shaking the saucepan gently, until the mixture is pulpy.

2 Transfer the mixture to a food processor or blender and process to a smooth purée. Push the purée through a sieve into a clean saucepan.

3 Add the stock and bring to the boil. Add the pasta, bring back to the boil and cook for 8-10 minutes, until the pasta is tender, but still firm to the bite. Season to taste with salt and pepper. Ladle into warmed bowls, sprinkle with the parsley and serve immediately.

Beans feature widely in Tuscan cuisine. This smooth, comforting soup, in which beans are simmered for 2 hours, is very simple to make. Garlic and parsley, stirred in just before serving, complement the flavour, and a drizzle of olive oil adds the final touch.

white bean soup
zuppa di fagioli

SERVES 4

175 g/6 oz dried cannellini beans, covered and soaked
    overnight in cold water

1.7 litres/3 pints chicken or vegetable stock

115 g/4 oz dried corallini, conchigliette piccole or other
    soup pasta

6 tbsp olive oil

2 garlic cloves, chopped finely

4 tbsp chopped fresh flat-leaved parsley

salt and pepper

1 Drain the soaked beans and place them in a large, heavy-based saucepan. Add the stock and bring to the boil. Partially cover the saucepan, lower the heat and simmer for 2 hours, until tender.

2 Transfer about half the beans and a little of the stock to a food processor or blender and process to a smooth purée. Return the purée to the saucepan and stir well to mix. Bring the soup back to the boil.

3 Add the pasta to the soup, bring back to the boil and cook for 10 minutes, until tender.

4 Meanwhile, heat 4 tablespoons of the olive oil in a small saucepan. Add the garlic and cook over a low heat, stirring frequently, for 4–5 minutes, until golden. Stir the garlic into the soup and add the parsley. Season to taste with salt and pepper and ladle into warmed soup bowls. Drizzle with the remaining olive oil and serve immediately.

variation

Substitute borlotti beans for the cannellini and cook for about 1½ hours in step 1.

beef soup with eggs
zuppa pavese

*Good-quality, home-made beef consommé is
essential for this unusual soup. It is best to make
it 24 hours in advance so that you can remove every
trace of fat from the surface of the consommé.*

SERVES 4

for the consommé

**500 g/1 lb 2 oz beef marrow bones, sawn into
   7.5-cm/3-inch pieces**

350 g/12 oz stewing beef, in 1 piece

1.4 litres/2¹/₂ pints water

4 cloves

2 onions, halved

2 celery sticks, chopped coarsely

8 peppercorns

1 bouquet garni

55 g/2 oz unsalted butter

4 slices fresh white bread

115 g/4 oz freshly grated Parmesan cheese

4 eggs

salt and pepper

1 First, make the consommé. Place the bones in a large,
heavy-based saucepan with the stewing beef on top.
Add the water and bring to the boil over a low
heat, skimming off all the scum that rises to the surface.
Pierce a clove into each onion half and add to the
saucepan with the celery, peppercorns and bouquet
garni. Partially cover and simmer very gently for 3 hours.
Remove the meat and simmer for a further hour.

2 Strain the consommé into a bowl and set aside to
cool. When completely cold, chill in the fridge for at
least 6 hours, preferably overnight. Carefully remove and
discard the layer of fat that has formed on the surface.
Return the consommé to a clean saucepan and heat
until almost boiling.

3 When you are ready to serve, melt the butter in a
heavy-based frying pan. Add the bread, 1 slice at a
time if necessary, and fry over a medium heat until crisp
and golden on both sides. Remove from the frying pan
and place one each in the base of 4 warmed soup bowls.

4 Sprinkle half the Parmesan over the fried bread.
Carefully break an egg* over each slice of fried
bread, keeping the yolks whole. Season to taste with
salt and pepper and sprinkle with the remaining
Parmesan. Carefully ladle the hot consommé into
the soup bowls and serve immediately.

*cook's tip
If you prefer, you could lightly poach the eggs before
adding them to the bowls.

seafood soup 43
zuppa di pesce

Full of delicious Mediterranean flavours, this soup is less heavy and much easier to make than its Provençal cousin bouillabaisse.

SERVES 4

4 tbsp olive oil

1 garlic clove, sliced

2 tbsp chopped fresh flat-leaved parsley

1 dried red chilli, whole

200 g/7 oz canned plum tomatoes, chopped

1 cod or haddock head

125 ml/4 fl oz dry white wine

850 ml/1¹/₂ pints boiling water

salt

450 g/1 lb monkfish fillet

280 g/10 oz live mussels

450 g/1 lb uncooked prawns

salt and pepper

4 slices sfilatino, or use French bread,
    each 2-cm/³/₄-inch thick

1 Heat half the olive oil in a large, heavy-based saucepan. Add the garlic, half the parsley and the chilli and cook over a low heat, stirring occasionally, for 3 minutes, until the garlic begins to colour. Add the tomatoes, fish head and wine and continue to cook until almost all the liquid has gone. Add the boiling water, season with salt and simmer for 20 minutes.

2 Meanwhile, remove the grey membrane from the monkfish and cut the flesh into bite-sized pieces. Scrub the mussels under cold running water and tug off the beards. Discard any mussels with broken or damaged shells and those that do not shut immediately when sharply tapped. Peel the prawns, cut a slit along the back of each and remove and discard the dark vein.

3 Add the monkfish and mussels to the saucepan and simmer for 4–5 minutes. Add the prawns and simmer for a further 2–3 minutes, until they have changed colour.

4 Remove and discard the fish head* and the chilli. Remove any mussels that have not opened. Add the remaining olive oil and parsley to the soup, taste and adjust the seasoning if necessary.

5 Toast the bread and put a slice in the base of 4 warmed soup bowls. Ladle the soup over the bread and serve immediately.

cook's tip
Italian cooks would probably slice off the cheeks from the fish head and add them to the soup.

Overleaf Sienna is situated in the centre of Tuscany. It is famous for its history and Gothic architecture

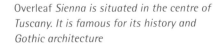

marinated raw beef
carpaccio

SERVES 4

200 g/7 oz fillet of beef, in 1 piece

2 tbsp lemon juice

salt and pepper

4 tbsp extra virgin olive oil

55 g/2 oz Parmesan cheese, shaved thinly

4 tbsp chopped fresh flat-leaved parsley

lemon slices, to garnish

ciabatta or focaccia, to serve

1 Using a very sharp knife, cut the beef fillet into wafer-thin slices and arrange on 4 individual serving plates.

2 Pour the lemon juice into a small bowl and season to taste with salt and pepper. Whisk in the olive oil, then pour the dressing over the meat. Cover the plates with clingfilm and set aside for 10–15 minutes to marinate.

3 Remove and discard the clingfilm. Arrange the Parmesan shavings in the centre of each serving and sprinkle with parsley. Garnish with lemon slices and serve with fresh bread.

variation

To make *Carpaccio di Tonno*, substitute fresh, uncooked tuna for the fillet of beef. Do not use thawed frozen fish, and eat on the day of purchase.

You need extremely thin slices of meat for this recipe. If you place the beef in the freezer for about 30 minutes, you will find it easier to slice.

prosciutto with rocket
prosciutto con la rucola

Rocket has become a fashionable salad vegetable in many homes and restaurants, but it has never been out of favour in Italy, where it grows wild.

SERVES 4

115 g/4 oz rocket

1 tbsp lemon juice

salt and pepper

3 tbsp extra virgin olive oil

225 g/8 oz prosciutto, sliced thinly

1 Separate the rocket leaves, wash in cold water and pat dry on kitchen paper. Place the leaves in a bowl.

2 Pour the lemon juice into a small bowl and season to taste with salt and pepper. Whisk in the olive oil, then pour the dressing over the rocket leaves and toss lightly so they are evenly coated.

3 Carefully drape the prosciutto in folds on 4 individual serving plates, then add the rocket. Serve at room temperature.

variation

For a more substantial salad, add 1 thinly sliced fennel bulb and 2 thinly sliced oranges to the rocket in step 1. Substitute orange juice or balsamic vinegar for the lemon juice in step 2.

48 # mixed antipasto meat platter
salumi

The town of San Daniele competes with Parma for the prize for the best cured ham (prosciutto), while Milan stakes its claim for the tastiest salami against stiff competition from Naples, Rome and Cremona. Let your taste buds be the judges.

SERVES 4

1 Cantaloupe melon

55 g/2 oz Italian salami, sliced thinly

8 slices prosciutto

8 slices bresaola

8 slices mortadella

4 plum tomatoes, sliced thinly

4 fresh figs, quartered

115 g/4 oz black olives*, stoned

2 tbsp shredded fresh basil leaves

4 tbsp extra virgin olive oil, plus extra for serving

pepper

1 Cut the melon in half, scoop out and discard the seeds, then cut the flesh into 8 wedges. Arrange the wedges on one half of a large serving platter.

2 Arrange the salami, prosciutto, bresaola and mortadella in loose folds on the other half of the platter. Arrange the tomato slices and fig quarters along the centre of the platter.

3 Scatter the olives over the meat. Sprinkle the basil over the tomatoes and drizzle with olive oil. Season to taste with pepper, then serve with extra olive oil.

*cook's tip

For extra flavour, make up your own marinated olives. Combine 450 g/1 lb stoned black olives, 1 sliced garlic clove, 1 red chilli, 3 slices lemon and 2 tablespoons red wine vinegar and mix well. Transfer to a screw-top jar and add sufficient extra virgin olive oil to cover. Screw on the lid and leave at room temperature for 2 weeks.

The Pantheon in Rome was built as a temple to the gods 2,000 years ago. It has a famous round opening, or oculus, in its roof

polenta with parma ham
polenta con prosciutto

These tasty morsels are ideal appetizers when you are entertaining, as they can be prepared in advance and then popped under the grill when you are ready to serve.

SERVES 6

600 ml/1 pint water

70 g/2¹/₂ oz quick-cook polenta

25 g/1 oz freshly grated Parmesan cheese

2 tbsp butter, softened

salt and ground black pepper

extra virgin olive oil, to serve

for the topping

2 tbsp extra virgin olive oil, plus extra for greasing

6 slices Parma ham or other prosciutto crudo

85 g/3 oz fontina cheese, cut into 6 slices

12 fresh sage leaves

1 Line a 15 x 25-cm/6 x 10-inch Swiss roll tin with baking parchment and set aside.

2 Pour the measured water into a large saucepan and bring to the boil. Reduce the heat so that it is just simmering and add a large pinch of salt. Add the polenta in a steady stream, stirring constantly. Simmer, stirring constantly, for 5 minutes, until thickened.

3 Remove the saucepan from the heat and stir in the Parmesan and butter and season to taste with pepper. Spoon the polenta evenly into the tin and smooth the surface with a palette knife. Set aside to cool completely.

4 Oil a baking sheet and a 7.5-cm/3-inch plain, round pastry cutter. Turn out the polenta, stamp out 6 rounds and place on the baking tray. Brush generously with a little olive oil and season with salt and pepper.

5 Cook under a preheated grill for 3-4 minutes. Turn the rounds over, brush with more oil and grill for a further 3-4 minutes, until golden. Remove from the grill and, if you are not serving immediately, set the rounds aside to cool completely.

6 Drape a slice of ham on each polenta round and top with a slice of fontina. Brush the sage leaves with some of the remaining olive oil and place 2 on each polenta round.

7 Cook the polenta rounds under a preheated grill for 3-4 minutes, until the cheese has melted and the sage is crisp. Serve immediately with extra olive oil for dipping.

variation

Substitute crumbled Gorgonzola cheese for the grated Parmesan.

52 roman artichokes
carciofi alla romana

The Roman contribution to this dish of stuffed artichokes is to flavour it with mint. Italian or Roman mint has a particularly sweet flavour, but you could use ordinary garden mint or one of the more exciting varieties, such as lemon or apple mint.

SERVES 4

5 tbsp lemon juice

4 globe artichokes

1 garlic clove

4 sprigs fresh flat-leaved parsley

2 sprigs fresh mint

1 lemon, quartered

4 tbsp olive oil

salt and pepper

2 tbsp dry, uncoloured breadcrumbs

2 garlic cloves, chopped finely

25 g/1 oz fresh flat-leaved parsley,
   chopped coarsely

25 g/1 oz fresh mint, chopped coarsely

1 tbsp unsalted butter, diced

1 Select a bowl large enough to accommodate the prepared artichokes and fill with cold water and 4 tablespoons of the lemon juice. Working on one artichoke at a time, snap off the stems, then peel away the tough outer leaves. Snip or break off the tough tops of the remaining leaves. When the central cone of the artichoke appears, cut off the top 2 cm/³/₄ inch with a sharp knife. Drop the prepared artichokes into the acidulated water to prevent them from discolouring.

2 Place the artichokes in a heavy-based saucepan that is large enough to hold them firmly upright in a single layer. Add the whole garlic clove, parsley sprigs, mint sprigs, lemon quarters and olive oil and season to taste with salt and pepper. Pour in sufficient water to come two-thirds of the way up the sides. Bring to the boil over a low heat, cover tightly and simmer for about 15 minutes, until nearly tender.

3 Meanwhile, combine the breadcrumbs, chopped garlic, parsley and mint in a bowl and season to taste with salt and pepper.

4 Remove the artichokes from the saucepan and set aside to cool slightly. When they are cold enough to handle, gently separate the leaves, remove the central bearded chokes or cones with a teaspoon and discard. Season the artichokes to taste with salt and pepper. Return them to the saucepan, again standing them upright in a single layer. Spoon the breadcrumb mixture into the centres, cover tightly and cook over a low heat for 20–30 minutes, until tender.

5 Using a slotted spoon, transfer the artichokes to 4 individual serving plates and set aside. Strain the cooking liquid into a clean saucepan and bring to the boil over a high heat. Cook until reduced by about one-quarter or until the juices are concentrated, then lower the heat and stir in the remaining lemon juice. Add the butter, a piece at a time, swirling the sauce in the saucepan until the butter has melted. Do not allow the sauce to boil. When all the butter has been incorporated, remove the saucepan from the heat. Serve the artichokes still warm and hand round the sauce separately.

54

warm vegetable medley
caponata

This melt-in-the-mouth mixture of tomatoes, aubergines and celery, flavoured with garlic and capers, is a traditional Sicilian appetizer.

SERVES 4

4 tbsp olive oil

2 celery sticks, sliced

2 red onions, sliced

450 g/1 lb aubergines, diced

1 garlic clove, chopped finely

5 plum tomatoes, chopped

3 tbsp red wine vinegar

1 tbsp sugar

3 tbsp green olives, stoned

2 tbsp capers*

salt and pepper

4 tbsp chopped fresh flat-leaved parsley

ciabatta or panini, to serve

1 Heat half the olive oil in a large, heavy-based saucepan. Add the celery and onions and cook over a low heat, stirring occasionally, for 5 minutes, until softened, but not coloured. Add the remaining oil and the aubergines. Cook, stirring frequently, for about 5 minutes, until the aubergines begin to colour.

2 Add the garlic, tomatoes, vinegar and sugar and mix well. Cover the mixture with a circle of greaseproof paper and simmer gently for about 10 minutes.

3 Remove the greaseproof paper, stir in the olives and capers and season to taste with salt and pepper. Tip the caponata into a serving dish and set aside to cool to room temperature. Sprinkle the parsley over the vegetables and serve with fresh bread or rolls.

*cook's tip

If possible, buy Sicilian capers for this dish. They are simply packed in salt and just need rinsing before use. Otherwise, use capers pickled in brine, but avoid those that are bottled in vinegar.

cheese and sun-dried tomato toasts
bruschetta

These tempting morsels make delicious canapés to serve with pre-dinner drinks or an excellent appetizer.

SERVES 4

2 sfilatini*

175 ml/6 fl oz sun-dried tomato purée

300 g/10¹/₂ oz mozzarella di bufala, drained and diced

1¹/₂ tsp dried oregano

2–3 tbsp olive oil

pepper

*cook's tip

If you are unable to find sfilatini, use a large ciabatta and cut the slices in half.

1 Slice the loaves diagonally and discard the end pieces. Toast the slices on both sides under a preheated grill until golden.

2 Spread one side of each toast with the sun-dried tomato purée and top with mozzarella. Sprinkle with oregano and season to taste with pepper.

3 Place the toasts on a large baking sheet and drizzle with olive oil. Bake in a preheated oven, 220°C/425°F/Gas Mark 7, for about 5 minutes, until the cheese has melted and is bubbling. Remove the hot toasts from the oven and leave them to stand for 5 minutes before serving.

56 # sicilian stuffed tomatoes
pomodori alla siciliana

1 Cut a thin slice off the tops of the tomatoes and discard. Scoop out the seeds with a teaspoon and discard, taking care not to pierce the shells. Turn the tomato shells upside down on kitchen paper to drain.

2 Heat 6 tablespoons of the olive oil in a frying pan, add the onions and garlic and cook over a low heat, stirring occasionally, for 5 minutes, until softened. Remove the frying pan from the heat and stir in the breadcrumbs, anchovies, olives and herbs.

3 Using a teaspoon, fill the tomato shells with the breadcrumb mixture, then place in an ovenproof dish large enough to hold them in a single layer. Sprinkle the tops with grated Parmesan and drizzle with the remaining oil.

4 Bake in a preheated oven, 180°C/350°F/Gas Mark 4, for 20-25 minutes, until the tomatoes are tender and the topping is golden brown.

5 Remove the dish from the oven and serve immediately, if serving hot, or leave to cool to room temperature.

A classic combination of sun-ripened tomatoes, black olives, anchovies and fresh herbs, this recipe is simplicity itself. It is best eaten, Italian-style, at room temperature, but you can serve it hot, if you prefer.

SERVES 4

8 large, ripe tomatoes

7 tbsp extra virgin olive oil

2 onions, finely chopped

2 garlic cloves, crushed

115 g/4 oz fresh breadcrumbs

8 anchovy fillets in oil, drained and chopped

3 tbsp black olives, stoned and chopped

2 tbsp chopped fresh flat-leaved parsley

1 tbsp chopped fresh oregano

4 tbsp freshly grated Parmesan cheese

Italy's Amalfi coast is made up of small fishing villages, such as Minori, that are situated on steep cliffs

58 # fried cheese sandwiches
mozzarella in carrozza

This Neapolitan speciality is one of the nicest ways to serve mozzarella cheese. It makes a wonderful snack for 2 people, as well as a superb appetizer for 4.

SERVES 4

for the sauce

3 tbsp olive oil

1 onion, chopped

2 garlic cloves, chopped finely

1 red pepper, deseeded and chopped

400 g/14 oz canned tomatoes, chopped

2 tbsp tomato purée

1 tbsp lemon juice

2 tbsp water

salt and pepper

200g /7 oz mozzarella di bufala

8 x 1-cm/¹/₂-inch thick slices day-old white bread, crusts removed

85 g/3 oz unsalted butter

4 medium slices Italian salami

corn oil, for deep-frying

3 eggs

3 tbsp milk

salt and pepper

1 First, make the sauce. Heat the olive oil in a medium, heavy-based saucepan. Add the onion and garlic and cook over a low heat, stirring occasionally, for 5 minutes, until softened. Add the red pepper and cook, stirring frequently, for a further 5 minutes. Stir in the tomatoes, tomato purée, lemon juice and water and season to taste with salt and pepper. Cover the saucepan and simmer for about 15 minutes, until pulpy.

2 Meanwhile, slice the mozzarella into 4 thick or 8 medium slices. Spread the bread slices with the butter and place the mozzarella on 4 of them. Top with the salami and sandwich together with the remaining slices of bread. Cut in half to make triangles, wrap in clingfilm and chill in the fridge.

3 Remove the sauce from the heat and set aside to cool slightly in the saucepan, then process in a food processor or blender until smooth. Return the sauce to a clean saucepan and reheat gently.

4 Heat the corn oil in a deep-fryer to 180–190°C/ 350–375°F or, if using a heavy-based saucepan, until a cube of day-old bread browns in 30 seconds. Meanwhile, beat the eggs with the milk in a shallow dish and season to taste with salt and pepper. Unwrap the sandwiches and dip them, in batches, into the egg mixture, allowing them to soak briefly. Add the sandwiches, in batches, to the hot oil and cook until golden brown on both sides. Remove with tongs, drain well on kitchen paper and keep warm while you cook the remaining triangles. Serve the sandwiches hot and hand round the sauce separately.

PASTA, RICE & PIZZA

Ask a room full of people to name an Italian dish and the chances are some would say pasta, others risotto and still others pizza. If you then asked the pasta lovers for a specific recipe, they would probably all name a different one – and so would aficionados of rice and pizza. In other words, these three are well-loved staples, not only in Italy, but throughout the world.

pasta

For many people, pasta is Italian cooking and most certainly it is served frequently and in almost every part of the country. Traditionally, it forms the first of two lunchtime courses, rather than being a main dish as is often the case outside Italy. As well as being inexpensive, filling and nourishing, pasta is immensely versatile and goes well with a vast range of ingredients – vegetables, mushrooms, meat, fish, seafood, herbs and cheese – or a simple drizzle of the best extra virgin olive oil. Sauces may be simple or elaborate, time-consuming or quick and easy, but, as with all Italian cooking, their success depends on using the best-quality and freshest ingredients.

The recipes each suggest a suitable pasta variety, but there is no reason why you shouldn't substitute your own favourites. For example, Bolognese Sauce (see page 70) is traditionally served with tagliatelle, but spaghetti is already a popular alternative and other ribbon pastas would work equally well. You could substitute a flavoured pasta for a plain one to create a more colourful dish or use a mixture for an attractive *tricolore* effect.

Baked pasta dishes, such as the classic *Lasagne al Forno* (see page 79), are heart-warming on a chilly

success depends on using the best-quality and freshest ingredients

winter's day, while simpler and lighter recipes, such as *Farfalle all'Alfredo* (see page 74) would be the perfect *primo* for an al fresco lunch. If speed is of the essence, what could be simpler than *Linguine alla Puttanesca* (see page 90)?

Fresh pasta is typical of northern Italy, while dried pasta is more usual in the south, but it is really a matter of personal taste which you prefer to use.

What is important is that it is cooked until it is just tender. It is a mistake to drain it too thoroughly and once cooked, it should be tossed immediately with the sauce or with a little butter or olive oil to prevent it from drying out.

The Colosseum in Rome is the most visited monument in Italy

64

how to cook pasta

There is a right way to cook pasta so that it is *al dente* – tender but still firm to the bite. Bring a large saucepan of lightly salted water to the boil. Add the pasta and bring the water back to the boil. Start timing as soon the water returns to the boil. Do not simmer pasta or it will become sticky – the water should be boiling fast, uncovered. Fresh pasta takes only a few minutes, while most dried pasta requires 8-10 minutes. However, cooking times can vary (check the packet instructions) and you should start testing about 2 minutes before you think it will be ready. The easiest way to test is to remove a small piece and bite it between your front teeth. If it is tender, but not soggy, the pasta is cooked. Drain it straight away and quickly in a colander. It is better if the pasta is not thoroughly drained. Immediately toss with the prepared sauce or with olive oil. Do not leave pasta standing before serving or it will become sticky and unappetizing. Some cooks add a tablespoon of olive oil to the cooking water to prevent the pasta from sticking. This is not necessary if there is plenty of water and it is boiling vigorously.

which pasta?

There are no fixed rules about which sauce partners which pasta shape, but there are traditional recipes and also a few helpful guidelines. Sauces that cling, such as those made with eggs, cream, grated cheese, olive oil, butter and herbs, are ideal with long thin pasta. Chunky sauces go well with pasta shapes that can hold them like tiny cups.

Plain dried pasta is off-white, while egg pasta has a more golden colour. Pasta may also be coloured and flavoured by adding other ingredients to the dough. Spinach (green) and tomato (red) are very common and, combined with plain pasta, make *pasta tricolore*. Green and yellow egg pasta ribbons are known as *paglia e fieno* – straw and hay. Squid or cuttlefish ink

produces dramatic-looking black pasta that contrasts superbly with shellfish for a dinner party, and beetroot produces a deep magenta colour. Other flavourings and colourings include porcini and other mushrooms, chillies and peppers. Wholemeal pasta in a limited number of shapes is also available.

long pasta

Bavette: narrow, oval pasta, popular in the south.
Bucatini: hollow pasta, slightly thicker than spaghetti. Popular in Sicily and Rome.
Capelli d'angelo: 'angel hair' pasta that is very fine and usually sold in nests. Typically used in soups or for serving to children.
Chitarra: 'guitar' pasta, so named after the wire strung wooden frames on which it is cut. It has a square cross-section.
Fettuccelle: straight, flat pasta ribbons.

Fettuccine: flat, quite narrow pasta ribbons, originally from Rome and still common in Lazio. Fettuccine are sold in nests.

Fusilli lunghi: long pasta like an extended corkscrew.

Lasagnette: wide, flat pasta. Lasagnette sometimes have wavy edges.

Linguine: 'little tongues'. Thin, spaghetti-like pasta.

Linguinette: very thin, spaghetti-like pasta.

Maccheroni: refers to long, thick, hollow pasta tubes in northern Italy, whereas in the south, the term usually refers to small pasta. Maccheroni is also used as a generic term for any pasta.

Nastroni: short, wide pasta ribbons, like shavings.

Pappardelle: wide pasta ribbons, which may have one wavy edge. Usually made from egg pasta.

Spaghetti: 'little strings'. Thin, hollow pasta tubes.

Spaghettini: very thin, hollow pasta tubes.

Tagliarini: flat pasta ribbons, thinner than tagliatelle.

Tagliatelle: flat pasta ribbons, originally from Bologna. Sold in nests.

Tonnarelli: flat pasta ribbons, similar to tagliatelle. Sold in nests.

Trenette: narrow ribbons, usually made from egg pasta and originally from the Liguria region, where they are traditionally served with the classic basil sauce, pesto.

Vermicelli: 'little worms'. Very fine, hollow pasta.

Zite: 'fiancées', so called because they were traditionally served at wedding celebrations in southern Italy. Long, thick, hollow tubes.

short pasta

There are hundreds of different shapes and even more names because the same shape may be called something different in another region. New shapes are being developed all the time.

Benfatti: 'well made', ironically so called because it consists of scraps and offcuts of pasta from making other shapes.

Chifferi: small, curved tubes, which may be ridged. Also called *chifferini*, *chifferoni* and *chifferotti*.

Conchiglie: shell-shaped pasta that is extremely popular because it traps sauces inside. Varies in size from tiny soup pasta to large shells that can be stuffed. *Conchiglie rigate* are ridged.

Eliche: 'propeller', so called because of their spiral shape. Eliche are easily confused with fusilli. Available in a range of sizes and colours.

Elicoidali: 'helixes'. Short, narrow, hollow pasta tubes, with curved ridges.

Farfalle: 'butterflies', this bow-shaped pasta is available in a range of colours and may be ridged.

Fusilli: 'rifles', so named because they are spirals that closely resemble the barrel of a gun in shape. They can be distinguished from eliche by the fact the spiral opens out, rather than remaining firm. Unlike eliche, fusilli are rarely coloured.

Garganelli: tubular egg pasta that has been rolled like a scroll. A speciality of Emilia-Romagna.

Gemelli: 'twins'. So called because two strips of pasta are twisted together.

Lumache: 'snails', shell-shaped pasta, that may be ridged (*lumache rigate*).

Maccheroni: small, hollow, bent pasta tubes. This usage is particularly common in southern Italy, whereas in the north, maccheroni usually refers to long pasta. The word is also used as a generic term for any pasta.

Orecchiette: 'little ears'. Small flat pasta shapes that are a speciality of Puglia. They have a chewy texture.

Penne: 'quills', so called because the hollow pasta tubes have diagonally cut ends, like a quill pen. They may be smooth (*penne lisce*) or ridged (*penne rigate*). Very popular both inside and outside Italy.

Pipe: 'pipes'. Small, hollow, bent pasta tubes. Most often available as *pipe rigate*, ridged tubes.

Rigatoni: chunky, hollow, ridged shapes that are slightly chewy.

Rotelle or Ruote: 'wheels', so called because they resemble cartwheels. Very popular with children and available in different colours. They are also known as *ruote di carro*.

Strozzapreti: 'priest stranglers', so called because they consist of two strands of pasta twisted together. The polite version of the story is that they got their name from a priest who liked them so much, he gobbled his food and choked. The more likely explanation lies in the historic hostility between church and state.

soup pasta

There are hundreds of tiny pasta shapes, called pastina, for adding to clear soups and broths.

Acini di pepe: 'peppercorns'.

Alfabeti: medium-sized, alphabet shapes, which are very popular with children.

Anellini: 'rings'. Small to medium hoops. Anellini are sometimes ridged.

Conchigliette: 'small shells'.

Farfalline: 'small butterflies'.

Fregola: tiny shapes resembling couscous. A speciality of Sardinia.

Funghetti: 'small mushrooms'.

Lumachine: 'small snails'.

Occhi: tiny pasta shapes.

Orecchiettini: 'tiny ears'.

Orzi: 'barley'.

Risi: 'rice'.

Semi di melone: 'melon seeds'.

Stelle: 'stars'. Medium-sized soup pasta.

Stellette: 'small stars'.

Tubetti: 'small tubes'.

pasta for baking

Pasta layered with meat, fish or vegetable sauce, coated in a creamy béchamel and sprinkled with cheese before baking in the oven is invariably made with lasagne or a variation of it. It can also be filled and rolled up before baking, rather like cannelloni.

Lasagne: dry pasta sheets that may be rectangular or square and plain, green or wholewheat. Some versions have curly edges. Traditional lasagne requires precooking before layering it in the dish. To precook: plunge 3 or 4 sheets into a large saucepan of lightly salted water and boil for about 8 minutes (check the packet instructions) until tender, but still firm to the bite. Remove with tongs and lay the sheets flat on a clean, damp tea towel, while you cook the remaining sheets. No-precook pasta can be layered straight from the packet, but the assembled dish may take longer to cook.

filled pasta

Agnolotti: half-moon shaped filled pasta, with a crinkled edge. A speciality of the Piedmont, they are traditionally filled with meat.

Cannelloni: 'large reeds'. Pasta tubes, which may

be plain, spinach or wholemeal. Use a teaspoon or piping bag to fill them. They are larger than ravioli or tortellini, so various fillings are possible.

Cappelletti: 'little hats'. Pasta squares are folded diagonally around a filling, then two of the ends are wrapped around an edge to make a brim. A speciality of Emilia-Romagna, they are traditionally filled with minced meat and cheese. They are served in clear broth at Christmas.

Pansotti: pasta squares are filled, then folded into triangles, with a bulge in the centre. A speciality of Liguria, they are traditionally filled with pecorino cheese, hard-boiled eggs and spinach and served with a walnut sauce.

Ravioli: all-purpose filled pasta, which are usually square, but may also be rectangular, round or oval. The edges are fluted. Ravioli are sometimes served in a clear broth.

Tortellini: pasta dough rounds are folded, then wrapped around a finger and the ends tucked in to resemble Venus's navel, apparently. A speciality of Bologna, they are traditionally filled with minced meat and prosciutto. Tortellini are served in a clear broth at Christmas.

Tortelloni: a larger version of tortellini.

rice

Rice is accorded much greater standing in Italy than it is in many other countries. It is never served plain or regarded as a mere accompaniment to more exciting ingredients. Risotto – meaning little rice – forms a course on its own, which is considered just as important as the meat or fish that is to follow. The dish was created to exploit the particular characteristics of Italian rice varieties and it is essential to use risotto rice to achieve the unique creamy texture. It is typical of Italian cooking that time and care are lavished on its preparation – you cannot hurry a risotto. The liquid should always be

Sauces that cling such as those made with eggs, cream, grated cheese, olive oil, butter and herbs, are ideal with long thin pasta

added a ladleful at a time and the risotto stirred constantly until it has all been absorbed.

Risottos may be based on a wide variety of ingredients – vegetables, seafood, mushrooms, chicken or cheese – but they are never made from leftovers. Some, such as *Risotto ai Quattro Formaggi* (see page 99), are wonderfully rich, while others, such as *Risotto alla Milanese* (see page 98), are deceptively simple. All are attractive and appetizing.

pizza

There can be few places in the world where the word pizza is unknown and these days you will find them with toppings that range from the basic to the bizarre. Traditional pizzas, however, rarely have a huge mass of ingredients that fight for the attention of our taste buds. In characteristic Italian style, a few harmonious and well-balanced flavours are preferred.

The classic cheese for pizza is mozzarella because of its superb melting qualities. It is no coincidence that the best mozzarella comes from the area around Naples, the city that invented the pizza. It is worth buying good-quality mozzarella, preferably one made from buffalo's milk. Try to avoid the semi-hard, yellow mozzarella, sometimes ready-grated and sold specifically for pizzas.

Overleaf *Numerous buildings in cities such as Venice have traditional façades that date back many centuries*

tagliatelle with a rich meat sauce
tagliatelle alla bolognese

One of the world's best-known and most-loved pasta dishes, Bologna's meat sauce – ragù – is classically served not with spaghetti, but with tagliatelle. Do use steak, not ordinary minced beef.

SERVES 4

4 tbsp olive oil, plus extra for serving

85 g/3 oz pancetta or rindless streaky bacon, diced

1 onion, chopped

1 garlic clove, chopped finely

1 carrot, chopped

1 celery stick, chopped

225 g/8 oz minced steak

115 g/4 oz chicken livers, chopped

2 tbsp passata

125 ml/4 fl oz dry white wine

225 ml/8 fl oz beef stock or water

1 tbsp chopped fresh oregano

1 bay leaf

salt and pepper

450 g/1 lb dried tagliatelle

freshly grated Parmesan cheese, to serve

1 Heat the olive oil in a large, heavy-based saucepan. Add the pancetta or bacon and cook over a medium heat, stirring occasionally, for 3–5 minutes, until it is just turning brown. Add the onion, garlic, carrot and celery and cook, stirring occasionally, for a further 5 minutes.

2 Add the steak and cook over a high heat, breaking up the meat with a wooden spoon, for 5 minutes, until browned. Stir in the chicken livers and cook, stirring occasionally, for a further 2–3 minutes. Add the passata, wine, stock, oregano and bay leaf and season to taste with salt and pepper. Bring to the boil, lower the heat, cover and simmer for 30–35 minutes*.

3 When the sauce is almost cooked, bring a large saucepan of lightly salted water to the boil. Add the pasta, bring back to the boil and cook for 8–10 minutes, until tender, but still firm to the bite. Drain, transfer to a warmed serving dish, drizzle with a little olive oil and toss well.

4 Remove and discard the bay leaf from the sauce, then pour it over the pasta, toss again and serve immediately with grated Parmesan.

*cook's tip
You can also layer this sauce with sheets of lasagne and Béchamel Sauce (see page 79) and bake the dish in the oven.

Pasta, rice and pizza form the basis of a menu at an Italian restaurant and the cuisine has now spread worldwide

spaghetti with meatballs
spaghetti con le polpette

Every Italian 'Mama' has her own version of this dish, which, naturally, is the very best.

SERVES 6

1 potato, diced

400 g/14 oz minced steak

1 onion, finely chopped

1 egg

4 tbsp chopped fresh flat-leaved parsley

plain flour, for dusting

5 tbsp virgin olive oil

400 ml/14 fl oz passata

2 tbsp tomato purée

400 g/14 oz dried spaghetti

salt and pepper

for the garnish

6 fresh basil leaves, shredded

freshly grated Parmesan cheese

1 Place the potato in a small pan, add cold water to cover and a pinch of salt and bring to the boil. Cook for 10-15 minutes, until tender, then drain. Either mash thoroughly with a potato masher or fork or pass through a potato ricer.

2 Combine the potato, steak, onion, egg and parsley in a bowl and season to taste with salt and pepper. Spread out the flour on a plate. With dampened hands, shape the meat mixture into walnut-size balls and roll in the flour. Shake off any excess.

3 Heat the oil in a heavy-based frying pan, add the meatballs and cook over a medium heat, stirring and turning frequently, for 8-10 minutes, until golden all over.

4 Add the passata and tomato purée and cook for a further 10 minutes, until the sauce is reduced and thickened.

5 Meanwhile, bring a large saucepan of lightly salted water to the boil. Add the pasta, bring back to the boil and cook for 8-10 minutes, until tender, but still firm to the bite.

6 Drain well and add to the meatball sauce, tossing well to coat. Transfer to a warm serving dish, garnish with the basil leaves and Parmesan and serve immediately.

74 # farfalle with cream and parmesan
farfalle all'alfredo

SERVES 4

450 g/1 lb dried farfalle

25 g/1 oz unsalted butter

150 ml/¼ pint double cream

pinch of freshly grated nutmeg

salt and pepper

to finish

4 tbsp double cream

55 g/2 oz freshly grated Parmesan cheese,
  plus extra to serve

This classic Roman dish is simplicity itself, but tastes just wonderful.

1 Bring a large saucepan of lightly salted water to the boil. Add the pasta, bring back to the boil and cook for 8–10 minutes, until tender, but still firm to the bite, then drain thoroughly.

2 Put the butter and cream in a large, heavy-based saucepan and bring to the boil. Lower the heat and simmer for 1 minute, until slightly thickened.

3 Add the drained pasta to the cream mixture. Place the saucepan over a low heat and toss until the farfalle are thoroughly coated. Season to taste with nutmeg, salt and pepper, then add the cream and grated Parmesan. Toss again and serve immediately with extra Parmesan for sprinkling.

variation

For a more substantial dish, melt the butter on its own in step 2 and add 350 g/12 oz petits pois. Cook for 2–3 minutes, add the cream and continue as above.

fusilli with gorgonzola and mushroom sauce
fusilli alla boscaiola

This aromatic pasta sauce sums up the Italian approach to cooking – a few, fairly basic ingredients, but they must be of the best quality possible.

SERVES 4

350 g/12 oz dried spaghetti

3 tbsp olive oil

350 g/12 oz wild mushrooms*, sliced

1 garlic clove, chopped finely

400 ml/14 fl oz double cream

250 g/9 oz Gorgonzola cheese, crumbled

salt and pepper

2 tbsp chopped fresh flat-leaved parsley, to garnish

1 Bring a large saucepan of lightly salted water to the boil. Add the pasta, bring back to the boil and cook for 8–10 minutes, until tender, but still firm to the bite.

2 Meanwhile, heat the olive oil in a heavy-based saucepan. Add the mushrooms and cook over a low heat, stirring frequently, for 5 minutes. Add the garlic and cook for a further 2 minutes.

3 Add the cream, bring to the boil and cook for 1 minute, until slightly thickened. Stir in the cheese and cook over a low heat until it has melted. Do not allow the sauce to boil, once the cheese has been added. Season to taste with salt and pepper and remove the saucepan from the heat.

4 Drain the pasta and tip it into the sauce. Toss well to coat, then serve immediately, garnished with the parsley.

*cook's tip

Wild mushrooms have a much earthier flavour than cultivated ones, so they complement the strong taste of the cheese. Porcini are especially delicious, but rather expensive. Field or Caesar's mushrooms, if you can find them, would also be a good choice. Otherwise, use cultivated mushrooms, but add 25 g/1 oz dried porcini, soaked for 20 minutes in 225 ml/8 fl oz hot water.

76 baked pasta with mushrooms
crostata ai funghi

A crostata may be a tart or, as in this case, a bake of pasta, béchamel sauce and a tasty filling.

SERVES 4

140 g/5 oz fontina cheese, sliced thinly

1 x quantity hot Béchamel Sauce (see page 79)

85 g/3 oz butter, plus extra for greasing

350 g/12 oz mixed wild mushrooms, sliced

350 g 12 oz dried tagliatelle

2 egg yolks

salt and pepper

4 tbsp freshly grated pecorino cheese

1 Stir the fontina cheese into the béchamel sauce and set aside.

2 Melt 25 g/1 oz of the butter in a large pan. Add the mushrooms and cook over a low heat, stirring occasionally, for 10 minutes.

3 Meanwhile, bring a large saucepan of lightly salted water to the boil. Add the pasta, bring back to the boil and cook for 8-10 minutes, until tender, but still firm to the bite. Drain, return to the saucepan and add the remaining butter, the egg yolks and about one-third of the sauce, then season to taste with salt and pepper. Toss well to mix, then gently stir in the mushrooms.

4 Lightly grease a large, ovenproof dish and spoon in the pasta mixture. Pour over the remaining sauce evenly and sprinkle with the grated pecorino.

5 Bake in a preheated oven, 200°C/400°F/Gas Mark 6, for 15-20 minutes, until golden brown. Serve immediately.

The Duomo, or cathedral, in Florence

1 First, make the meat sauce. Heat the olive oil in a
large, heavy-based saucepan. Add the onion, celery,
carrot, pancetta, beef and pork and cook over a medium
heat, stirring frequently and breaking up the meat with
a wooden spoon, for 10 minutes, until lightly browned.

2 Add the wine, bring to the boil and cook until reduced.
Add about two-thirds of the stock, bring to the boil
and cook until reduced. Combine the remaining stock
and tomato purée and add to the saucepan. Season to
taste, add the clove and the bay leaf and pour in the
milk. Cover and simmer over a low heat for 1½ hours.

3 Next, make the béchamel sauce. Melt the butter, add
the flour and cook over a low heat, stirring constantly,
for 1 minute. Remove the saucepan from the heat and
gradually stir in the milk. Return the saucepan to the
heat and bring to the boil, stirring constantly, until
thickened and smooth. Add the bay leaf and simmer
gently for 2 minutes. Remove the bay leaf and season
the sauce to taste with salt, pepper and nutmeg.
Remove the saucepan from the heat and set aside.

4 Unless you are using lasagne that needs no
precooking, bring a large saucepan of lightly salted
water to the boil. Add the lasagne sheets, in batches,
bring back to the boil and cook for about 10 minutes,
until tender, but still firm to the bite. Remove with
tongs and spread out on a clean tea towel.

5 Remove the meat sauce from the heat and discard
the clove and bay leaf. Lightly grease a large, ovenproof dish with butter. Place a layer of lasagne in the
base and cover it with a layer of meat sauce. Spoon a
layer of béchamel sauce on top and sprinkle with one-
third of the mozzarella and Parmesan cheeses. Continue
making layers until all the ingredients are used, ending
with a topping of béchamel sauce and sprinkled cheese.

6 Dot the top of the lasagne with the diced butter
and bake in a preheated oven, 200°C/400°F/Gas
Mark 6, for 30 minutes, until golden and bubbling.

baked lasagne
lasagne al forno

79

*You need plenty of time to make a baked lasagne
with an authentic flavour, but it is worth it.*

SERVES 4

for the meat sauce

3 tbsp olive oil

1 onion, chopped finely

1 celery stick, chopped finely

1 carrot, chopped finely

100 g/3½ oz pancetta or rindless streaky bacon,
  chopped finely

175 g/6 oz minced beef

175 g/6 oz minced pork

100 ml/3½ fl oz dry red wine

150 ml/¼ pint beef stock

1 tbsp tomato purée

salt and pepper

1 clove

1 bay leaf

150 ml/¼ pint boiling milk

for the Béchamel Sauce

55 g/2 oz unsalted butter

55 g/2 oz plain flour

500 ml/18 fl oz milk

1 bay leaf

salt and pepper

pinch of freshly grated nutmeg

400 g/14 oz dried lasagne verdi

140 g/5 oz mozzarella cheese, drained and diced

140 g/5 oz freshly grated Parmesan cheese

55 g/2 oz unsalted butter, diced, plus extra for greasing

cannelloni with spinach and ricotta
cannelloni imbottiti

Creamy ricotta cheese and spinach is a favourite Italian combination that appears in many guises. This pasta dish originated in the Emilia-Romagna region.

SERVES 4

12 dried cannelloni tubes, 7.5-cm/3-inches long

butter, for greasing

for the filling

140 g/5 oz lean ham*, chopped

140 g/5 oz frozen spinach, thawed and drained

115 g/4 oz ricotta cheese

1 egg

3 tbsp freshly grated pecorino cheese

pinch of freshly grated nutmeg

salt and pepper

for the cheese sauce

600 ml/1 pint milk

25 g/1 oz unsalted butter

2 tbsp plain flour

85 g/3 oz freshly grated Gruyère cheese

salt and pepper

1 Bring a large saucepan of lightly salted water to the boil. Add the cannelloni tubes, bring back to the boil and cook for 6–7 minutes, until nearly tender. Drain and rinse under cold water. Spread out the tubes on a clean tea towel.

2 Put the ham, spinach and ricotta into a food processor and process for a few seconds until combined. Add the egg and pecorino and process again to a smooth paste. Scrape the filling into a bowl and season to taste with nutmeg, salt and pepper.

3 Grease an ovenproof dish with butter. Spoon the filling into a piping bag fitted with a 1-cm/½-inch nozzle. Carefully open one cannelloni tube, stand it upright and pipe in the filling. Place the filled tube in the dish and continue to fill the remaining cannelloni.

4 To make the cheese sauce, heat the milk to just below boiling point. Meanwhile, melt the butter in another saucepan. Add the flour to the butter and cook over a low heat, stirring constantly, for 1 minute. Remove the saucepan from the heat and gradually stir in the hot milk. Return the saucepan to the heat and bring to the boil, stirring constantly. Simmer over the lowest possible heat, stirring frequently, for 10 minutes, until thickened and smooth. Remove the saucepan from the heat, stir in the Gruyère and season to taste with salt and pepper.

5 Spoon the cheese sauce over the filled cannelloni. Cover the dish with foil and bake in a preheated oven, 180°C/350°F/Gas Mark 4, for 20–25 minutes. Serve immediately.

*cook's tip

For a vegetarian version of this dish, simply omit the ham or substitute the same weight of mushrooms.

*Globe artichokes grow wild in Sicily and are
cultivated throughout Italy, but they are always
considered a speciality of Roman cooking.*

SERVES 4

2 tbsp lemon juice

4 baby globe artichokes

7 tbsp olive oil

2 shallots, chopped finely

2 garlic cloves, chopped finely

2 tbsp chopped fresh flat-leaved parsley

2 tbsp chopped fresh mint

350 g/12 oz dried rigatoni or other tubular pasta

12 large uncooked prawns*

25 g/1 oz unsalted butter

salt and pepper

1 Fill a bowl with cold water and add the lemon juice.
Prepare the artichokes one at a time. Cut off the stems
and trim away any tough outer leaves. Cut across the
tops of the leaves. Slice in half lengthways and remove
the central fibrous chokes, then cut lengthways into
5-mm/¼-inch thick slices. Immediately place the slices
in the bowl of acidulated water to prevent discoloration.

2 Heat 5 tablespoons of the olive oil in a heavy-based
frying pan. Drain the artichoke slices and pat dry
with kitchen paper. Add them to the frying pan with the
shallots, garlic, parsley and mint and cook over a low
heat, stirring frequently, for 10–12 minutes, until tender.

3 Meanwhile, bring a large saucepan of lightly salted
water to the boil. Add the pasta, bring back to the
boil and cook for 8–10 minutes, until tender, but still
firm to the bite.

4 Peel the prawns, cut a slit along the back of each
and remove and discard the dark vein. Melt the
butter in a small frying pan, cut the prawns in half
and add them to the frying pan. Cook, stirring
occasionally, for 2–3 minutes, until they have changed
colour. Season to taste with salt and pepper.

5 Drain the pasta and tip it into a bowl. Add the
remaining olive oil and toss well. Add the
artichoke mixture and the prawns and toss again.
Serve immediately.

*cook's tip
The large Mediterranean prawns, known as *gamberoni*
in Italy, have a superb flavour and texture that is superior
to that of the very big tiger prawns, but they may be
difficult to obtain.

Overleaf *Vineyards are very much part of rural Italy*

rabid pasta 87
pasta all'arrabbiata

The pasta is 'arrabbiata' – rabid or angry – because it is red hot with fiery chillies. This dish is a speciality of the province of Lazio.

SERVES 4

for the sugocasa
5 tbsp extra virgin olive oil
450 g/1 lb plum tomatoes, chopped
salt and pepper

150 ml/5 fl oz dry white wine
1 tbsp sun-dried tomato paste
2 fresh red chillies
2 garlic cloves, chopped finely
350 g/12 oz dried tortiglioni
4 tbsp chopped fresh flat-leaved parsley
salt and pepper
shavings of pecorino cheese, to garnish

1 First make the sugocasa.* Heat the olive oil in a frying pan until it is almost smoking. Add the tomatoes and cook over a high heat for 2-3 minutes. Reduce the heat to low and cook gently for 20 minutes, or until very soft. Season with salt and pepper, then pass through a food mill into a clean saucepan.

2 Add the wine, tomato paste, whole chillies and garlic to the sugocasa and bring to the boil. Lower the heat and simmer gently.

3 Meanwhile, bring a large saucepan of lightly salted water to the boil. Add the pasta, bring back to the boil and cook for 8-10 minutes, until tender, but still firm to the bite.

The church at Capella

4 Meanwhile, remove the chillies and taste the sauce. If you prefer a hotter flavour, chop some or all of the chillies and return them to the saucepan. Check the seasoning at the same time then stir in half the parsley.

5 Drain the pasta and tip it into a warm serving bowl. Add the sauce and toss to coat. Sprinkle with the remaining parsley, garnish with the pecorino shavings and serve immediately.

*cook's tip
If time is short, use ready-made sugocasa, available from most supermarkets and sometimes labelled crushed tomatoes. Failing that, you could use passata, but the sauce will be thinner.

radiatori with pumpkin sauce
radiatori al sugo di zucca

Long, slow cooking results in a marvellous melding of sweet flavours in the pumpkin sauce in this southern dish.

SERVES 4

for the sauce

55 g/2 oz unsalted butter

115 g/4 oz white onions or shallots, chopped very finely

salt

800 g/1 lb 12 oz pumpkin, unprepared weight

pinch of freshly grated nutmeg

350 g/12 oz dried radiatori

200 ml/7 fl oz single cream

4 tbsp freshly grated Parmesan cheese, plus extra
  to serve

2 tbsp chopped fresh flat-leaved parsley

salt and pepper

1 Melt the butter in a heavy-based saucepan over a low heat. Add the onions, sprinkle with a little salt, cover and cook, stirring frequently, for 25–30 minutes.

2 Scoop out and discard the seeds from the pumpkin. Peel and finely chop the flesh. Tip the pumpkin into the saucepan and season to taste with nutmeg. Cover and cook over a low heat, stirring occasionally, for 45 minutes.

3 Meanwhile, bring a large saucepan of lightly salted water to the boil. Add the pasta, bring back to the boil and cook for 8–10 minutes, until tender, but still firm to the bite. Drain thoroughly, reserving about 150 ml/¼ pint of the cooking liquid.

4 Stir the cream, grated Parmesan and parsley into the pumpkin sauce and season to taste with salt and pepper. If the mixture seems a little too thick, add some or all of the reserved cooking liquid. Tip in the pasta and toss for 1 minute. Serve immediately, with extra Parmesan for sprinkling.

variation

Although traditionally made with pumpkin, you could also use butternut or acorn squash for this dish.

90

linguine with anchovies, olives and capers
linguine alla puttanesca

This flavoursome Neapolitan dish takes its name from the Italian word puttana, *meaning a prostitute, but no one seems quite sure why.*

SERVES 4

for the sauce

3 tbsp olive oil

2 garlic cloves, chopped finely

10 anchovy fillets*, drained and chopped

140 g/5 oz black olives, stoned and chopped

1 tbsp capers, rinsed

450 g/1 lb plum tomatoes, peeled (see page 36), deseeded and chopped

pinch of cayenne pepper

salt

400 g/14 oz dried linguine

2 tbsp chopped fresh flat-leaved parsley, to garnish

1 Heat the olive oil in a heavy-based saucepan. Add the garlic and cook over a low heat, stirring frequently, for 2 minutes. Add the anchovies and mash them to a pulp with a fork. Add the olives, capers and tomatoes and season to taste with cayenne pepper. Cover and simmer for 25 minutes.

2 Meanwhile, bring a saucepan of lightly salted water to the boil. Add the pasta, bring back to the boil and cook for 8–10 minutes, until tender, but still firm to the bite. Drain and transfer to a warmed serving dish.

3 Spoon the anchovy sauce into the dish and toss the pasta, using 2 large forks. Garnish with the parsley and serve immediately.

*cook's tip

Salted anchovies have a much better flavour than canned fillets, but are not so widely available. If you can find them, soak them in cold water for 30 minutes, then pat dry with kitchen paper before using.

seafood pasta parcels
spaghetti ai frutti di mare al cartoccio

Although not a long-standing tradition, baking parcels of mixed ingredients in the oven has now become a favourite Italian cooking technique. It is especially well suited to seafood, as it seals in the moisture and keeps it tender.

SERVES 4

1.5 kg/3 lb 5 oz crab, cooked freshly

2 tbsp virgin olive oil

2 fresh red chillies, deseeded and chopped finely

4 garlic cloves, chopped finely

800 g/1 lb 12 oz canned tomatoes

225 ml/8 fl oz dry white wine

salt and pepper

350 g/12 oz dried spaghetti

450 g/1 lb live mussels

2 tbsp butter

115 g/4 oz prepared squid, sliced (see page 181)

175 g/6 oz uncooked Mediterranean prawns

3 tbsp coarsely chopped fresh flat-leaved parsley

1 tbsp shredded fresh basil leaves

1 Holding the crab upright with one hand, bang it firmly on the underside of the shell with your clenched fist to loosen the body. Then, with the shell towards you and still holding it upright, force the body away from the shell by pushing with your thumbs. Twist off and discard the tail. Twist off the legs and claws. Crack them open and remove all the meat.

2 Pull off and discard the gills - dead man's fingers - then split open the body down the centre using a sharp knife. Remove all the meat, discarding any pieces of shell. Reserve all the shell and set the crab meat aside. Carefully break up the larger pieces of shell with a meat mallet or the end of a rolling pin.

3 Heat 1 tablespoon of the olive oil in a large saucepan. Add half the chillies and half the garlic, then add the pieces of crab shell. Cook over a medium

heat, stirring occasionally, for 2–3 minutes. Add the tomatoes with their can juices and the wine. Lower the heat and simmer for about 1 hour. Strain the sauce, pressing down on the contents of the sieve with a wooden spoon. Season to taste with salt and pepper and set aside.

4 Bring a large saucepan of lightly salted water to the boil. Add the pasta, bring back to the boil and cook for 8-10 minutes, until tender, but still firm to the bite.

5 Scrub and debeard the mussels under cold running water. Discard any damaged or broken ones or those that do not shut immediately when sharply tapped.

6 Heat the remaining oil with the butter in a large, heavy-based saucepan. Add the remaining chilli and garlic and cook over a low heat, stirring occasionally, for 5 minutes, until softened. Add the squid, prawns and mussels, cover and cook over a high heat for 4-5 minutes, until the mussels have opened. Remove the saucepan from the heat and discard any mussels that remain closed.

7 Drain the pasta and add it to the seafood with the chilli and tomato sauce, parsley and basil, tossing well to coat.

8 Cut out 4 large squares of baking parchment or greaseproof paper. Divide the pasta and seafood among them, placing it on one half. Fold over the other half and turn in the edges securely to seal. Transfer to a large baking sheet and bake in a preheated oven, 180°C/350°F/Gas Mark 4, for about 10 minutes, until the parcels have puffed up. Serve immediately.

layered spaghetti with smoked salmon and prawns
pasticcio di spaghetti con salmone affumicato e gamberoni

Now enjoying considerable popularity in fashionable restaurants in many cities both in Italy and elsewhere in the world, pasta and smoked salmon is quite a recent partnership. This is quite a special dish, but astonishingly easy to make.

SERVES 6

70 g/2¹/₂ oz butter, plus extra for greasing
350 g/12 oz dried spaghetti
200 g/7 oz smoked salmon, cut into strips
280 g/10 oz large Mediterranean prawns or tiger prawns,
  cooked, peeled and deveined
1 x quantity Béchamel Sauce (see page 79)
115 g/4 oz freshly grated Parmesan cheese
salt

1 Butter a large, ovenproof dish and set aside.

2 Bring a large saucepan of lightly salted water to the boil. Add the pasta, bring back to the boil and cook for 8-10 minutes, until tender, but still firm to the bite. Drain well, return to the saucepan, add 55 g/2 oz of the butter and toss well.

3 Spoon half the spaghetti into the prepared dish, cover with the strips of smoked salmon, then top with the prawns. Pour over half the béchamel sauce and sprinkle with half the Parmesan. Add the remaining spaghetti, cover with the remaining sauce and sprinkle with the remaining Parmesan. Dice the remaining butter and dot it over the surface.

4 Bake in a preheated oven, 180°C/350°F/Gas Mark 4, for 15 minutes, until the top is golden. Serve immediately.

variation
This dish would also be delicious made with smoked halibut instead of the salmon and smoked mussels instead of the prawns.

Narrow alley in Gubbio

SERVES 4

1 kg/2 lb 4 oz live clams

175 ml/6 fl oz water

175 ml/6 fl oz dry white wine

350 g/12 oz dried spaghetti

5 tbsp olive oil

2 garlic cloves, chopped finely

4 tbsp chopped fresh flat-leaved parsley

salt and pepper

equipment

1 square of muslin

In Italy, this dish would be prepared with small, smooth-shelled clams, known as vongole, *but you can use other varieties, such as Venus clams. If fresh clams are not available, substitute 280 g/10 oz of clams in brine, which are sold in jars.*

spaghetti with clams 97
spaghetti alla vongole

1 Scrub the clams under cold running water and discard any with broken or damaged shells or those that do not shut when sharply tapped. Place the clams in a large, heavy-based saucepan, add the water and wine, cover and cook over a high heat, shaking the saucepan occasionally, for 5 minutes, until the shells have opened.

2 Remove the clams with a slotted spoon and set aside to cool slightly. Strain the cooking liquid through a muslin-lined sieve into a small saucepan. Bring to the boil and cook until reduced by about half and remove from heat. Meanwhile, discard any clams that have not opened, remove the remainder from their shells and set aside.

3 Bring a large saucepan of lightly salted water to the boil. Add the pasta, bring back to the boil and cook for 8–10 minutes, until tender, but still firm to the bite.

4 Meanwhile, heat the olive oil in a large, heavy-based frying pan. Add the garlic and cook, stirring frequently, for 2 minutes. Add the parsley and the reduced cooking liquid and simmer gently.

5 Drain the pasta and add it to the frying pan with the clams. Season to taste with salt and pepper and cook, stirring constantly, for 4 minutes, until the pasta is coated and the clams have heated through. Transfer to a warmed serving dish and serve immediately.*

cook's tip
Don't be tempted to serve Parmesan for sprinkling: cheese really doesn't marry well with this pasta recipe.

Gondolas in Venice

98
saffron risotto
risotto alla milanese

SERVES 4

pinch of saffron threads

4 tbsp boiling water

1.2 litres/2 pints chicken or vegetable stock

85 g/3 oz unsalted butter

2 onions, chopped finely

2 garlic cloves, chopped finely

350 g/12 oz arborio rice

150 ml/¼ pint dry white wine

85 g/3 oz freshly grated Parmesan cheese

salt and pepper

The saffron (giallo) in what is probably Italy's best-known rice dish is very eye-catching. Its delicate flavour makes it an ideal primo, or first course.

1 Place the saffron in a small bowl and add the boiling water. Set aside to soak. Pour the stock into a large saucepan and bring to the boil. Lower the heat and simmer gently.

2 Melt 55 g/2 oz of the butter in another large, heavy-based saucepan. Add the onions and garlic and cook over a low heat, stirring occasionally, for 5 minutes, until softened. Add the rice and cook, stirring, until all the grains are coated and glistening.

3 Add the wine and cook, stirring constantly, until it has almost completely evaporated. Add a ladleful of the hot stock and cook, still stirring constantly, until all the stock has been absorbed. Continue cooking, stirring and adding the stock, a ladleful at a time, for about 20 minutes*, or until the rice is tender and all the liquid has been absorbed.

4 Add the saffron liquid, the remaining butter and the Parmesan and season to taste with salt and pepper. Cook for 1–2 minutes, until heated through, then serve immediately.

*cook's tip
It is essential to stir the rice constantly for at least the first 10 minutes of cooking in the stock and it is safer to do so throughout the whole cooking time. However, as you become a more experienced risotto cook, you will recognize the 'feel' of the rice and can stir frequently, rather than constantly, for the last 10 minutes.

risotto with four cheeses
risotto ai quattro formaggi

1 Pour the stock into a large saucepan and bring to the boil. Lower the heat and simmer gently.

2 Melt the butter in another large, heavy-based saucepan. Add the onion and cook over a low heat, stirring occasionally, for 5 minutes, until softened. Add the rice and cook, stirring constantly, for 2–3 minutes, until all the grains are thoroughly coated and glistening.

3 Add the wine and cook, stirring constantly, until it has almost completely evaporated. Add a ladleful of the hot stock and cook, stirring constantly, until all the stock has been absorbed. Continue cooking, stirring and adding the stock, a ladleful at a time, for about 20 minutes, or until the rice is tender and the liquid has been absorbed.*

4 Remove the saucepan from the heat and stir in the Gorgonzola, taleggio, fontina and about one quarter of the Parmesan until melted. Season to taste with salt and pepper. Transfer the risotto to a warmed serving dish, sprinkle with the remaining Parmesan, garnish with the parsley and serve immediately.

This is a very rich primo *that would probably be served at a special occasion dinner or to guests. Taleggio and fontina are wonderful melting cheeses that give the dish its creamy consistency.*

SERVES 6

1 litre/1³/₄ pints vegetable stock

40 g/1¹/₂ oz unsalted butter

1 onion, chopped finely

350 g/12 oz arborio rice

200 ml/7 fl oz dry white wine

55 g/2 oz Gorgonzola cheese, crumbled

55 g/2 oz freshly grated taleggio cheese

55 g/2 oz freshly grated fontina cheese

55 g/2 oz freshly grated Parmesan cheese

salt and pepper

2 tbsp chopped fresh flat-leaved parsley, to garnish

*cook's tip

There is a saying in Italy that for a perfect creamy risotto, the rice should just catch on the base of the saucepan. Nevertheless, it is important to use a heavy-based saucepan to prevent the rice from sticking and burning.

seafood risotto
risotto alla marinara

Every town in the rice-growing regions of northern Italy has its own speciality risotto – this is Venice's.

1 Peel the prawns, reserving the head and shells, and cut a slit along the back of each and remove and discard the dark vein, then reserve until required. Scrub the mussels and clams under cold running water and debeard the mussels. Discard any damaged or broken shellfish or those that do not shut immediately when sharply tapped. Wrap the prawn heads and shells in a square of muslin and pound gently with a pestle or the side of a rolling pin, reserving any liquid they may yield.

2 Place the garlic, lemon, mussels and clams in a large, heavy-based saucepan and add the muslin-wrapped shells and any reserved liquid. Pour in the water, cover tightly and bring to the boil over a high heat. Cook, shaking the saucepan frequently, for 5 minutes, until the shellfish have opened. Discard any that remain closed. Transfer the mussels and clams to a bowl and strain the cooking liquid through a muslin-lined sieve into a measuring jug. Make up the amount of liquid to 1.2 litres/2 pints with water.

3 Pour this liquid into a clean saucepan. Bring to the boil, then lower the heat and simmer gently.

4 Melt 25 g/1 oz of the butter with the olive oil in another large, heavy-based saucepan. Add the onion and half the parsley and cook over a low heat, stirring occasionally, for 5 minutes, until softened. Add the rice and cook, stirring constantly, for 2–3 minutes, until all the grains are coated and glistening.

5 Add the wine and cook, stirring constantly, until it has almost completely evaporated. Add a ladleful of

SERVES 4

225 g/8 oz uncooked prawns

225 g /8 oz live mussels

225 g/8 oz live clams

2 garlic cloves, halved

1 lemon, sliced

600 ml/1 pint water

115 g/4 oz unsalted butter

1 tbsp olive oil

1 onion, chopped finely

2 tbsp chopped fresh flat-leaved parsley

350 g/12 oz arborio rice

125 ml/4 fl oz dry white wine

225 g /8 oz prepared squid, cut into small pieces (see page 181), or squid rings

4 tbsp Marsala

salt and pepper

equipment
2 squares of muslin

the hot stock and cook, still stirring constantly, until all the stock has been absorbed. Continue cooking, stirring and adding the stock, a ladleful at a time, for about 20 minutes, or until the rice is tender and all the liquid has been absorbed.

6 About 5 minutes before the rice is ready, melt 55 g/2 oz of the remaining butter in a heavy-based saucepan. Add the squid and cook, stirring frequently, for 3 minutes, then add the reserved prawns and cook for a further 2–3 minutes, until the squid is opaque and the prawns have changed colour. Stir in the Marsala, bring to the boil and cook until all the liquid has evaporated.

7 Stir the squid, prawns, mussels and clams into the rice, add the remaining butter and parsley and season to taste with salt and pepper. Heat through briefly and serve immediately.

102 rice and peas
risi e bisi

This famous and rather pretty dish is one of many risotti *from the Veneto.*

SERVES 4

1 litre/1¾ pints chicken or vegetable stock

85 g/3 oz butter

3 shallots, chopped finely

115 g/4 oz pancetta or rindless streaky bacon, diced

280 g/10 oz arborio rice

150 ml/¼ pint dry white wine

225 g/8 oz petits pois, thawed if using frozen

salt and pepper

Parmesan cheese shavings, to garnish

1 Pour the stock into a large saucepan and bring to the boil. Lower the heat and simmer gently.

2 Melt 55 g/2 oz of the butter in another large, heavy-based saucepan. Add the shallots and pancetta or bacon and cook over a low heat, stirring occasionally, for 5 minutes, until the shallots are softened. Add the rice and cook, stirring constantly, for 2–3 minutes, until all the grains are thoroughly coated and glistening.

3 Pour in the wine and cook, stirring constantly, until it has almost completely evaporated. Add a ladleful of hot stock and cook, stirring constantly, until all the stock has been absorbed. Continue cooking and adding the stock, a ladleful at a time, for about 10 minutes.

4 Add the peas, then continue adding the stock, a ladleful at a time, for about a further 10 minutes, or until the rice is tender and the liquid has been absorbed.

5 Stir in the remaining butter and season to taste with salt and pepper. Transfer the risotto to a warmed serving dish, garnish with Parmesan shavings and serve immediately.

variation

You can substitute diced cooked ham for the pancetta or bacon and add it towards the end of the cooking time so that it heats through.

pizza turnover
calzone

A calzone is a kind of inside-out pizza with the filling on the inside of the crust. This is a traditional cheese and vegetable recipe, but you could use almost any favourite pizza topping.

SERVES 4

2 x quantity Pizza Dough (see page 105)

plain flour, for dusting

for the filling

2 tbsp olive oil

1 red onion, sliced thinly

1 garlic clove, chopped finely

400 g/14 oz canned tomatoes, chopped

55 g/2 oz black olives, stoned

salt and pepper

200 g/7 oz mozzarella cheese, drained and diced

1 tbsp chopped fresh oregano

1 Heat the olive oil in a frying pan. Add the onion and garlic and cook over a low heat, stirring occasionally, for 5 minutes, until softened. Add the tomatoes and cook, stirring occasionally, for a further 5 minutes. Stir in the olives and season to taste with salt and pepper. Remove the frying pan from the heat.

2 Divide the dough into 4 pieces. Roll out each piece on a lightly floured surface to form a 20-cm/8-inch round.

3 Divide the tomato mixture among the rounds, spreading it over half of each almost to the edge. Top with the cheese and sprinkle with the oregano. Brush the edge of each round with a little water and fold over the uncovered sides. Press the edges to seal.

4 Transfer the turnovers to lightly oiled baking sheets and bake in a preheated oven, 200°C/400°F/Gas Mark 6, for about 15 minutes, until golden and crisp. Remove from the oven and leave to stand for 2 minutes, then transfer to warmed plates and serve.

cheese and tomato pizza
pizza margherita

With its red, white and green ingredients – the colours of the Italian flag – this pizza was created to honour Queen Margherita. While it is delicious with just this simple topping, it can also be used as a basis for more elaborate pizzas with extra ingredients.

SERVES 2

for the dough

225 g/8 oz plain flour, plus extra for dusting

1 tsp salt

1 tsp easy-blend dried yeast

1 tbsp olive oil, plus extra for brushing

6 tbsp lukewarm water

for the topping

6 tomatoes, sliced thinly

175 g/6 oz mozzarella cheese, drained and sliced thinly

salt and pepper

2 tbsp shredded fresh basil leaves

2 tbsp olive oil

1 To make the pizza dough, sift the flour and salt into a bowl and stir in the yeast. Make a well in the centre and pour in the oil and water. Gradually incorporate the dry ingredients into the liquid, using a wooden spoon or floured hands.

2 Turn out the dough on to a lightly floured surface and knead well for 5 minutes, until smooth and elastic. Return to the clean bowl, covered with lightly oiled clingfilm and set aside to rise in a warm place for about 1 hour, or until doubled in size.

3 Turn out the dough onto a lightly floured surface and knock back. Knead briefly, then cut it in half and roll out each piece into a round about 5 mm/ ¼ inch thick. Transfer to a lightly oiled baking sheet and push up the edges with your fingers to form a small rim.

4 For the topping, arrange the tomato and mozzarella slices alternately over the pizza bases. Season to taste with salt and pepper, sprinkle with the basil and drizzle with the olive oil.

5 Bake in a preheated oven, 230°C/450°F/Gas Mark 8, for 15–20 minutes, until the crust is crisp and the cheese has melted. Serve immediately.

variation

For Pizza Napoletana, first spread each pizza base with 4½ teaspoons tomato purée, then top with the tomato and cheese slices. Arrange halved, drained, canned anchovy fillets in a pattern on top, season to taste with pepper, drizzle with olive oil and bake as above.

four seasons pizza
pizza quattro stagioni

This pizza is divided into 4 sections, each with a different topping, to represent the 4 seasons. You can vary the toppings according to taste.

SERVES 2

1 x quantity Pizza Dough (see page 105)

plain flour, for dusting

for the tomato sauce

2 tbsp olive oil

1 small onion, chopped finely

1 garlic clove, chopped finely

1 red pepper, deseeded and chopped

225 g/8 oz plum tomatoes, peeled (see page 36) and chopped

1 tbsp tomato purée

1 tsp soft brown sugar

1 tbsp shredded fresh basil leaves

1 bay leaf

salt and pepper

for the topping

70 g/2¹/₂ oz drained bottled clams or drained anchovy fillets, halved lengthways, or cooked peeled prawns

55 g/2 oz baby globe artichokes or artichoke hearts, sliced thinly, or canned asparagus spears, drained

25 g/1 oz mozzarella cheese, drained and sliced thinly

1 tomato, sliced thinly

100 g/3¹/₂ oz mushrooms or pepperoni, sliced thinly

2 tsp capers, rinsed

2 tsp stoned, sliced black olives

2 tbsp olive oil, plus extra for brushing

salt and pepper

1 To make the tomato sauce, heat the olive oil in a heavy-based saucepan. Add the onion, garlic and pepper and cook over a low heat, stirring occasionally, for 5 minutes, until softened. Add the tomatoes, tomato purée, sugar, basil and bay leaf and season to taste with salt and pepper. Cover and simmer, stirring occasionally, for 30 minutes, until thickened. Remove the saucepan from the heat and set the sauce aside to cool completely.

2 Turn out the prepared pizza dough onto a lightly floured surface and knock back. Knead briefly, then cut it in half and roll out each piece into a round about 5 mm/¹/₄ inch thick. Transfer to a lightly oiled baking sheet and push up the edges with your fingers to form a small rim.

3 Spread the tomato sauce over the pizza bases, almost to the edge. Cover one quarter with clams, anchovy fillets or prawns. Cover a second quarter with sliced artichokes, artichoke hearts or asparagus spears. Cover the third quarter with alternate slices of mozzarella and tomato. Cover the final quarter with sliced mushrooms or pepperoni. Sprinkle the surface with capers and olives, season to taste with salt and pepper and drizzle with the olive oil.

4 Bake in a preheated oven, 220°C/425°F/Gas Mark 7, for 20–25 minutes, until the crust is crisp and the cheese has melted. Serve immediately.

variation

Other toppings, either used in combination or singly, could include: mixed seafood, such as prawns, mussels and squid rings; roasted Mediterranean vegetables, say aubergines, peppers, tomatoes, courgettes and red onions; wild mushrooms and pine kernels; or hot pepperoni and chillies.

seafood pizza
pizza alla marinara

SERVES 2

1 x quantity Pizza Dough (see page 105)

plain flour, for dusting

virgin olive oil, for greasing and drizzling

1 x quantity Tomato Sauce (see page 106)

225 g/8 oz mixed fresh* seafood, including cooked
   prawns, cooked mussels and squid rings

1/2 red pepper, deseeded and chopped

1/2 yellow pepper, deseeded and chopped

1 tbsp capers, rinsed

55 g/2 oz taleggio cheese, grated

3 tbsp freshly grated Parmesan cheese

1/2 tsp dried oregano

75 g/2¾ oz anchovy fillets in oil,
   drained and sliced

10 black olives, stoned

salt and pepper

1 Turn out the prepared pizza dough onto a lightly
floured surface and knock back. Knead briefly, then
roll out the dough into a round about 5 mm/¼ inch
thick. Transfer to a lightly oiled baking sheet and push
up the edge with your fingers to form a small rim.

2 Spread the tomato sauce over the pizza base,
almost to the edge. Arrange the mixed seafood, red
and yellow peppers and capers evenly on top.

3 Sprinkle the taleggio, Parmesan and oregano evenly
over the topping. Add the anchovy fillets and
olives, drizzle with olive oil and season to taste with
salt and pepper.

4 Bake in a preheated oven, 220°C/425°F/Gas Mark 7,
for 20-25 minutes, until the crust is crisp and the
cheese has melted. Serve immediately.

cook's tip
If you have to use frozen mixed seafood, make sure
it is completely thawed first.

*Bags of fresh mixed seafood, containing prawns,
squid rings, mussels and other shellfish are available
from the chiller cabinets of many supermarkets.
They tend to have a better flavour and texture than
frozen seafood.*

MEAT & POULTRY

112 Meat and poultry dishes traditionally fall into two categories – those for the rich and those for the poor. The former used the best cuts of meat from animals raised on lush pastures, often steak and veal. The latter, which were eaten less frequently, had to rely on tenderizing poorer cuts by long, slow cooking techniques. Both are equally delicious.

Italians do not eat a great deal of meat in comparison with some of their neighbours, and this is a contributing factor to the healthiness of their diet. They are also frugal and little is wasted, so offal also forms an important part of their meat intake. Liver is popular, especially tender calf's liver, while chicken livers are often used to top pasta or crostini. Kidneys, brains and sweetbreads form several regional specialities and tripe is cooked everywhere. Oxtail, calf's head, pig's trotter and calf's foot all have a role in traditional dishes.

By far the most popular meat in Italy is veal, a passion that is shared by few other nations with such intensity apart from the French. It is eaten in every region and recipes are innumerable. Calves are slaughtered at different ages to produce meat with different qualities, the best and most expensive being the very young *vitello di latte*, mainly produced in Lombardy and the Piedmont. Veal is served in a variety of ways: as *scallopine* (escalopes) and *piccate* (extra thin escalopes); *osso bucco*, made with shin of

Nothing of the animal is wasted – that which is not used for roasts, casseroles, stews, ham and bacon is converted into salami, cured meats and sausages

veal, and as *Vitello Tonnato* (see page 143) – thinly sliced cold roast veal served with a tuna sauce.

As with many peasant cultures, owning a pig is a way of life for many Italians. Nothing of the animal is wasted – that which is not used for roasts, casseroles, stews, ham and bacon is converted into salami, cured meats and sausages. The offal is an important food source, while even the snout and the tail have their uses. Fresh pork is cooked in various ways, from roasted loin to fillet in sweet-and-sour sauce.

Lamb features in southern Italian recipes and is an especially popular meat in Lazio, the area surrounding Rome. Like veal, the quality and character of lamb depends upon the age at which the animal is

Ponte Vecchio on the River Arno, Florence

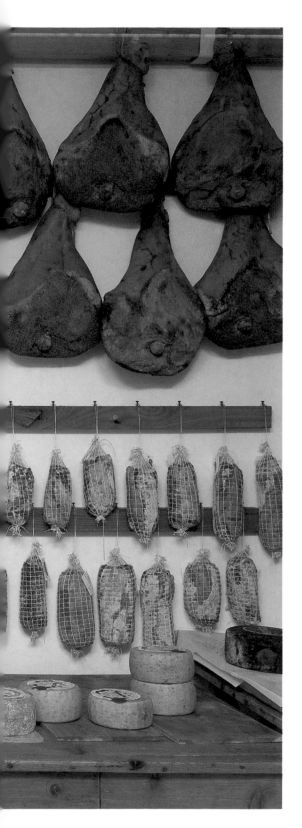

slaughtered. The youngest, most tender and succulent is known as *abbacchio*. Roast lamb is traditional on Easter Sunday, but there are many recipes for cutlets and braised lamb.

Beef in Italy is extremely variable. Tuscan beef ranks among the finest in the world, but meat from the south is usually far less tender and lean, mainly because the animals are not primarily bred for food, but for working on the farm. Meat sauces for pasta and meatballs are made from minced beef; rump and fillet steak are grilled; topside is sliced and rolled around a stuffing mixture; and less tender cuts are braised or stewed. *Carpaccio* (see page 46) is a famous dish of very thinly sliced raw fillet of beef, served as an antipasto.

Chicken is a popular and inexpensive source of meat in almost every country in the world and here Italy is no exception. As a general rule, it is cut into serving portions or boned and cut into bite-sized pieces before cooking, rather than roasted or braised whole. Most chicken in Italy is still free range.

Turkey, duck and goose also appear in various forms, the last often cooked with fruit to balance the richness of the meat. Most chicken recipes are interchangeable with turkey.

Furred and feathered game has a long history in Italian cuisine and still plays an important role in the daily menus of the southern regions in particular. Italians have been keen hunters for centuries and many continue to exercise a blatant disregard for the close season. One result of this is the increasing rarity of wild boar, once a standard dish in Tuscany and Sardinia. Young boar are cooked in the same way as pork, while older specimens are marinated for as long as 24 hours before roasting or braising.

Italy's cured meats are famous the world over. Cured ham and salami hang on this wall

116

Rabbit and hare are stewed, braised or cooked in many of the same ways as chicken, often served with fried polenta. Farmed rabbit has a more delicate flavour than wild specimens and is widely available. Hare, however, cannot be farmed and so always has a rich, gamey flavour. Both rabbit and hare are popular in sweet-and-sour sauce and are usually well marinated in red wine and herbs before cooking.

At one time, thousands of quail were shot as they migrated to Italy for the summer months, but now they have become something of a rarity. Most quail is farmed these days and has a milder, but still gamey flavour.

Although technically classed as game, guinea fowl have been farmed throughout Europe for centuries. They are about the size of a small chicken and have a similar but stronger flavour. They can be cooked in many of the same ways, including stuffed and roasted, casseroled and pot-roasted.

Italians are enthusiastic about the robust flavour of wild pigeon. As these birds can be quite tough, they are usually served braised or stewed. A classic Tuscan dish is to marinate pigeons and then braise them with tomatoes and olives. Domestic pigeons are raised on many farms and while their flavour is less robust they are generally far more tender than wild birds, making them suitable for roasting.

cured meats and sausages

The versatile and near-ubiquitous pig is the source of wonderful hams, salami, sausages and other cured meats. Many are still home-made in farmhouses and an enormous range of the commercial products are prepared by time-honoured methods. Virtually every region has its own specialities.

Prosciutto, for which Italy is world famous, is a salted, air-cured ham that is best eaten raw, often as an antipasto, although it can be briefly cooked and is an essential ingredient in *saltimbocca*. The best-known prosciutto, or Parma ham, is produced in a legally defined area around the city of Parma between the rivers Baganzo and Taro. It comes from pigs that have been fed on the whey produced during the process of making Parmesan cheese, which gives it a sweet, mild flavour. The ham is quite fatty, as the pigs are reared indoors and not allowed to roam freely. San Daniele in Friuli also produces a fine, air-cured prosciutto considered by some to have a better flavour than Parma ham. As the pigs are kept outdoors, the flesh is usually leaner. Prosciutto is also produced in several other places. It should be sliced wafer-thin and eaten within a day of purchase to prevent it from drying out.

Prosciutto cotto is cooked ham. It has usually been boiled and may be flavoured with herbs. It is widely used for sandwiches and snacks.

Bresaola, a speciality of Lombardy, is the beef equivalent of prosciutto, best made from thinly sliced fillet, salted then air-dried for several months. Cheaper bresaola is made from leg of beef and is less tender. Bresaola is less salty with a more delicate flavour than ham and is usually served as an antipasto with a little olive oil and lemon juice. Like prosciutto, buy it in wafer-thin slices and eat as soon after purchase as possible.

Pancetta is a kind of bacon made from salted and spiced belly of pork. Unsmoked pancetta is usually sold in round, rolled slices, while the smoked version is more often sold in thin strips. It adds a surprising depth of flavour to pasta sauces, casseroles and stews and is one of the main ingredients of *spaghetti alla carbonara*. It is widely available from Italian delicatessens. Streaky bacon makes a reasonable substitute, as pancetta is quite fatty.

Salami is cured pork sausage that may be eaten raw or used for pizza toppings. There are many different varieties and local specialities, with varying proportions of lean and fat meat and a selection of seasonings and flavourings. Among the most common is the fat-speckled *salame milano*, which includes minced beef as well as pork and is flavoured with white wine, garlic and pepper. It is mass-produced and not held in especially high regard. Parma's *salame di Felino*, on the other hand, is very lightly cured and has a delicate flavour that is particularly fine. It is also quite expensive. *Salame sardo*, from Sardinia, and *salame napoletano*, from Naples, are both spiced with red and black pepper. Tuscany's version, *salame fiorentino*, is flavoured with fennel seeds.

Other cured meats are produced in many regions and one of the best-known and most instantly recognizable is mortadella from Bologna. This large, mild, smooth sausage should be made from pure pork, but cheaper versions may include all kinds of other meat and non-meat products. Although it is naturally

a pale pink colour, studded with cubes of creamy fat, avoid brilliant pink mortadella, which will have been coloured artificially. Mortadella is nearly always eaten cold in sandwiches or as part of an antipasto, but it may be diced and added to pasta sauces and risotto.

Bologna is the city most associated with Italian cooking sausages, although they are produced in an immense variety in every region of the country. In addition to mass-produced sausages, there are also many small sausage shops, selling their own varieties flavoured with local produce from fresh herbs to wild mushrooms. Most sausages are made from coarsely chopped pork that is high in fat, but the speciality ones may be made from venison or wild boar.

Coppa, a dried and salted shoulder of pork sausage, is a speciality of Emilia-Romagna and Lombardy. It is irregular in shape, although tending towards the rectangular, deep red in colour and cased in natural skin. In Rome, the term coppa refers to a kind of brawn, rather than a sausage.

Cotechino is a lightly spiced and salted pork sausage from Lombardy, Emilia-Romagna and the Veneto. Weighing 1 kg/2 lb 4 oz, it is a large sausage cased in a skin – *coteca* means skin. It is an essential ingredient in *Bollito Misto* (see page 122) and is also served boiled and sliced with beans or lentils.

Luganega, from northern Italy, is a long, coiled pork sausage that is sold by length. It may be grilled or pan-fried and served with mashed potatoes or lentils. It can also be cut into chunks and stirred into risotto.

Zampone, often an ingredient in *Bollito Misto*, is a stuffed pig's trotter, weighing 1.5–2 kg/3 lb 5 oz– 4 lb 8 oz. When it is bought raw it needs to be boiled at home for 2–3 hours, or it can be purchased partially cooked and vacuum-packed. Zampone is sliced before serving with lentils or mashed potato.

Overleaf A typical old Italian town illuminated at night

lamb shanks with roasted onions 139
agnello alla perugina

Slow-roasted lamb is infused with the flavours of garlic and rosemary and served with sweet red onions and glazed carrot batons. You won't require anything more except a bottle of fruity red wine.

SERVES 4

4 x 350 g/12 oz lamb shanks

6 garlic cloves

2 tbsp virgin olive oil

1 tbsp very finely chopped fresh rosemary

pepper

4 red onions

salt 350 g/12 oz carrots, cut into thin batons

4 tbsp water

1 Trim off any excess fat from the lamb. Using a small, sharp knife, make 6 incisions in each shank. Cut the garlic cloves lengthways into 4 slices. Insert 6 garlic slices in the incisions in each lamb shank.

2 Place the lamb in a single layer in a roasting tin, drizzle with the olive oil, sprinkle with the rosemary and season with pepper. Roast in a preheated oven, 180°C/350°F/Gas Mark 4, for 45 minutes.

3 Wrap each of the onions in a square of foil. Remove the roasting tin from the oven and season the lamb shanks with salt. Return the tin to the oven and place the wrapped onions on the shelf next to it. Roast for a further 1-1¼ hours, until the lamb is very tender.

4 Meanwhile, bring a large saucepan of water to the boil. Add the carrot batons and blanch for 1 minute. Drain and refresh under cold water.

5 Remove the roasting tin from the oven when the lamb is meltingly tender and transfer it to a warmed serving dish. Skim off any fat from the roasting tin and place it over a medium heat. Add the carrots and cook for 2 minutes, then add the water, bring to the boil and simmer, stirring constantly and scraping up the glazed bits from the base of the roasting tin.

6 Transfer the carrots and sauce to the serving dish. Remove the onions from the oven and unwrap. Cut off and discard about 1 cm/½ inch of the tops and add the onions to the dish. Serve immediately.

140

roast lamb with rosemary and marsala
agnello al rosmarino e marsala

Serving tender spring lamb on Easter Sunday to celebrate the end of the Lenten fast is traditional throughout the Mediterranean, not least in Italy.

SERVES 6

1.8 kg/4 lb leg of lamb

2 garlic cloves, sliced thinly

2 tbsp rosemary leaves

8 tbsp olive oil

salt and pepper

900 g/2 lb potatoes, cut into 2.5 cm/1 inch cubes

6 fresh sage leaves, chopped

150 ml/¼ pint Marsala

1 Use a small, sharp knife to make incisions all over the lamb, opening them out slightly to make little pockets. Insert the garlic slices and about half the rosemary leaves in the pockets.

2 Place the lamb in a roasting tin and spoon half the olive oil over it. Roast in a preheated oven, 220°C/425°F/Gas Mark 7, for 15 minutes.

3 Lower the oven temperature to 180°C/350°/Gas Mark 4. Remove the lamb from the oven and season to taste with salt and pepper. Turn the lamb over, return to the oven and roast for a further hour.

4 Meanwhile, spread out the cubed potatoes in a second roasting tin, pour the remaining olive oil over them and toss to coat. Sprinkle with the remaining rosemary and the sage. Place the potatoes in the oven with the lamb and roast for 40 minutes.

5 Remove the lamb from the oven, turn it over and pour over the Marsala. Return it to the oven with the potatoes and cook for a further 15 minutes.

6 Transfer the lamb to a carving board and cover with foil. Place the roasting tin over a high heat and bring the juices to the boil. Continue to boil until thickened and syrupy. Strain into a warmed sauce boat or jug.

7 Carve the lamb into slices and serve with the potatoes and sauce.

146
veal with prosciutto and sage
saltimbocca alla romana

Originally from Brescia, but now a Roman speciality, saltimbocca literally means 'jump in the mouth', a reflection of just how highly regarded this dish is.

1 Place the veal escalopes between 2 sheets of clingfilm and pound with the flat end of a meat mallet or the side of a rolling pin until they are very thin. Transfer to a plate and sprinkle with the lemon juice. Set aside for 30 minutes, spooning the juice over them occasionally.

2 Pat the escalopes dry with kitchen paper, season with salt and paper and rub with half the sage. Place a slice of prosciutto on each escalope and secure with a cocktail stick.

3 Melt the butter in a large, heavy-based frying pan. Add the remaining sage and cook over a low heat, stirring constantly, for 1 minute. Add the escalopes and cook for 3–4 minutes on each side, until golden brown. Pour in the wine and cook for a further 2 minutes.

4 Transfer the escalopes to a warmed serving dish and pour the pan juices over them. Remove and discard the cocktail sticks and serve immediately.

variation
You can also prepare skinned, boned chicken breasts in the same way. If they are very thick, cut them in half first.

SERVES 4
4 veal escalopes

2 tbsp lemon juice

salt and pepper

1 tbsp chopped fresh sage leaves

4 slices prosciutto

55 g/2 oz unsalted butter

3 tbsp dry white wine

equipment
cocktail sticks

chicken with smoked ham and parmesan 147
pollo alla bolognese

There is much more to the cuisine of Bologna than the eponymous pasta dish, as it is renowned for its rich dishes. The capital of the Emilia-Romagna region, Bologna is nicknamed la grassa *– the fat, rich and plentiful one.*

SERVES 4

4 skinned, boned chicken breasts

2 tbsp plain flour

salt and pepper

55 g/2 oz unsalted butter

8 thin slices smoked ham, trimmed

55 g/2 oz freshly grated Parmesan cheese

fresh basil sprigs, to garnish

1 Cut each chicken breast through the thickness to open them out, then place the pieces between 2 sheets of clingfilm and pound with the flat end of a meat mallet or the side of a rolling pin until they are as thin as possible. Spread out the flour on a shallow plate and season with salt and pepper. Coat the chicken pieces in the seasoned flour, shaking off any excess.

2 Melt half the butter in a large, heavy-based frying pan. Add the chicken pieces, in batches if necessary, and cook over a medium heat, turning frequently, for 10–15 minutes, until golden brown all over and cooked through.

3 Meanwhile, melt the remaining butter in a small saucepan. Remove the frying pan containing the chicken from the heat. Place a slice of ham on each piece of chicken and sprinkle with the cheese. Pour the melted butter over the chicken and return the frying pan to the heat for 3–4 minutes, until the cheese has melted. Serve immediately, garnished with basil sprigs.

variation

A similar dish is made in the Valle d'Aosta, but instead of the chicken breasts being cut and opened out, they are slit to make a pocket. The pockets are then filled with slices of smoked ham or prosciutto and fontina cheese before frying.

148 # chicken in red wine with polenta
pollo al barolo

This richly flavoured and colourful stew from the Piedmont region is typically served with fried polenta for a delicious and filling meal.

Serves 4

for the polenta

1.5 litres/2³/₄ pints chicken stock or water

salt

300 g/10¹/₂ oz polenta*

5 tbsp olive oil

for the stew

3 tbsp olive oil

8 skinned chicken drumsticks or 4 skinned, boned
  chicken breasts

1 red onion, cut into thin wedges

2 tbsp sun-dried tomato pesto

300 ml/¹/₂ pint Barolo or other red wine

300 ml/¹/₂ pint chicken stock

salt and pepper

140 g/5 oz black grapes

equipment

28 x 18 cm/11 x 7 inch shallow tin

1 First, make the polenta. Bring the stock or water to the boil in a large saucepan. Add a pinch of salt, then gradually add the polenta in a steady stream, stirring constantly, with a wooden spoon. Simmer, stirring constantly, for about 30 minutes, until the mixture is very thick and comes away from the sides of the saucepan. Remove the saucepan from the heat.

2 Thoroughly grease the shallow tin with some of the olive oil. Spoon the polenta into the tin and spread it out evenly using a wet spatula. Set aside for at least 2 hours to cool and become firm.

3 To cook the stew, heat 2 tablespoons of the olive oil in a large, heavy-based saucepan. Add the chicken and cook over a medium heat, turning occasionally, for 5–7 minutes, until golden all over. Remove the chicken from the saucepan and set aside.

4 Add the remaining olive oil to the saucepan. When it is hot, add the onion and pesto and cook over a low heat, stirring, for 5 minutes, until the onion has softened. Stir in the wine and stock and bring to the boil.

5 Return the chicken to the saucepan and season to taste with salt and pepper. Lower the heat, cover and simmer, stirring occasionally, for 20–25 minutes, until the chicken is tender.

6 Meanwhile, cut the set polenta into squares. Heat the remaining olive oil in a large, heavy-based frying pan. Add the polenta, in batches if necessary. Cook the squares, turning frequently, for about 5 minutes, until golden brown all over. Remove from the frying pan, drain on kitchen paper and keep warm.

7 Halve the grapes lengthways and remove any seeds. Add them to the chicken and cook for a few minutes to heat through. Serve the stew immediately with the polenta.

***cook's tip**

If you prefer, you can use quick-cook polenta, which takes only about 5 minutes to prepare.

lombardy duck
anatra alla lombardia

Rich meat, such as duck and goose, is combined with pulses in the cuisines of many countries and Italy is no exception. This is a wonderfully flavoursome dish that would be a good choice when entertaining as it can be prepared in advance and gently reheated.

SERVES 4

for the stock

1 celery stick

1 garlic clove

6 peppercorns, crushed lightly

1 bay leaf

5 sprigs flat-leaved parsley

1 onion

1 clove

salt

2.25 kg/5 lb duck

225 g/8 oz small brown lentils

1 tbsp virgin olive oil

2 onions

2 celery sticks

2 tbsp brandy or grappa

150 ml/5 fl oz dry white wine

salt and pepper

1 tsp cornflour

1 Cut the duck into joints. Cut off the wings. Fold back the skin at the neck end and cut out the wishbone with a small, sharp knife. Using poultry shears or heavy kitchen scissors, cut the duck breast in half along the breastbone, from the tail end to the neck. Cut along each side of the backbone to separate the 2 halves. Remove the backbone. Cut each portion in half diagonally.

2 To make the stock, place the wings, backbone and neck, if available, in a large saucepan and add the celery, garlic, peppercorns, bay leaf and parsley. Stick the onion with the clove and add to the saucepan with a large pinch of salt. Add cold water to cover and bring to the boil. Skim off any scum that rises to the surface. Then lower the heat and simmer very gently for 2 hours. Strain into a clean saucepan and boil until reduced and concentrated. Measure 150 ml (5 fl oz) and reserve all the stock.

3 Rinse and pick over the lentils, then place in a saucepan. Pour in sufficient cold water to cover and add the olive oil. Cut 1 onion in half and add with 1 celery stick. Bring to the boil over medium heat, then lower the heat and simmer for about 15 minutes, until the lentils are just beginning to soften. Drain and reserve.

4 Meanwhile, put the duck portions, skin side down, in a heavy-based frying pan and cook, gently shaking the frying pan occasionally, for about 10 minutes. Transfer the duck portions to a flameproof casserole and drain off the excess fat from the frying pan.

5 Finely chop the remaining onion and celery and add to the frying pan. Cook over a low heat, stirring occasionally, for 5 minutes, until softened. Using a slotted spoon, transfer the vegetables to the casserole.

6 Set the casserole over a medium heat, add the brandy and ignite. When the flames have died down, add the wine and the reserved measured stock. Bring to the boil, add the lentils and season to taste with salt and pepper. Cover and simmer gently over a low heat for 40 minutes, until the duck and lentils are tender.

7 Combine the cornflour with 2 tablespoons of the stock to a smooth paste in a small bowl. Stir the paste into the casserole and cook, stirring frequently, for about 5 minutes, until thickened. Taste and adjust the seasoning, if necessary, and serve immediately.

500 kg/1,100 lb. However, the fish is usually sold cut into steaks, which may be grilled, barbecued, baked in the oven or cut into chunks and threaded onto skewers. The flesh can dry out easily, so it is best cooked with olive oil, tomatoes and other classic Mediterranean ingredients.

Sicilian fishermen have been catching tuna for centuries. This large, oily fish, usually sold as fillets or steaks, combines superbly with robust Mediterranean flavours, such as olives and capers. In the past, the traditional Arab tuna hunt, the *mantaza*, resulted in a huge glut of fish, which inspired Ignazio Florio to can it. Preserved in oil, brine, tomato sauce or any other, canned tuna is ideal for salads, sandwiches, vegetable stuffings and snacks of all kinds.

Red mullet is a delicious fish with a delicate flavour, which is sometimes compared to that of prawns. It can be grilled, baked or cooked in a parcel – a favourite Italian method – and marries well with olives, olive oil, tomatoes, herbs, saffron and garlic. Scaling red mullet is a time-consuming process, but worth the effort as it reveals the wonderful colouring. All Europeans regard the liver as a delicacy, so it is not removed when the fish is cleaned.

The variety of sea bream found off the Italian shores is the gilt head. This is a relatively large fish, with delicate, flavoursome, flaky white flesh. It is usually grilled or cooked in a parcel. For best flavour and texture, marinate the fish before cooking.

Sea bass has always been popular in Mediterranean cuisines, but it is only relatively recently that this fine fish has become fashionable elsewhere. The flesh is delicate and the fish is best grilled, pan-fried or barbecued whole. It is also very good stuffed and baked in the oven. In Italy, sea bass is caught wild, but the farmed fish is widely available in other countries.

Venetians have an excellent supply of seafood, including shellfish not found outside of the Lagoon

162

swordfish with olives and capers
pesce spada alla palermitana

SERVES 4

2 tbsp plain flour

salt and pepper

4 x 225 g/8 oz swordfish steaks

100 ml/3¹/₂ fl oz olive oil

2 garlic cloves, halved

1 onion, chopped

4 anchovy fillets, drained and chopped

4 tomatoes, peeled (see page 36), deseeded
  and chopped

12 green olives, stoned and sliced

1 tbsp capers, rinsed

fresh rosemary leaves, to garnish

*Swordfish is plentiful in the waters surrounding
Sicily, where it is usually cooked with traditional
Mediterranean ingredients. The recipe takes its name
from Palermo, Sicily's main port.*

1 Spread out the flour on a plate and season with
salt and pepper. Coat the fish in the seasoned flour,
shaking off any excess.

2 Gently heat the olive oil in a large, heavy-based
frying pan. Add the garlic and cook over a low heat
for 2–3 minutes, until just golden. Do not allow it to
turn brown or burn. Remove the garlic and discard.

3 Add the fish to the frying pan and cook over a
medium heat for about 4 minutes on each side,
until cooked through and golden brown. Remove the
steaks from the frying pan and set aside.

4 Add the onion and anchovies to the frying pan and
cook, mashing the anchovies with a wooden spoon
until they have turned to a purée and the onion is
golden. Add the tomatoes and cook over a low heat,
stirring occasionally, for about 20 minutes, until the
mixture has thickened.

5 Stir in the olives and capers and taste and adjust
the seasoning. Return the steaks to the frying pan
and heat through gently. Serve garnished with rosemary.

*Back street in Venice, with the
campanile of a church in the background*

178 # red mullet cooked in a parcel
triglie al cartoccio

Red mullet is a popular fish in Italy, not just because of its wonderful taste, but also because it looks so attractive. This is an ideal way of cooking it.

SERVES 4

4 tbsp extra virgin olive oil, plus extra for brushing

4 x 280 g/10 oz red mullet, cleaned and scaled, heads on

salt and pepper

4 garlic cloves, sliced thinly lengthways

4 tomatoes, peeled (see page 36), deseeded and diced

2 tsp finely chopped fresh rosemary

fresh bread, to serve

1 Cut 4 squares of greaseproof paper large enough to enclose the fish and brush with a little olive oil.

2 Rinse the fish inside and out under cold running water and pat dry with kitchen paper. Season. Using a sharp knife, cut 3 diagonal slits in both sides of each fish. Insert the garlic slices into the slits.

3 Combine the olive oil, tomatoes and rosemary in a bowl. Spoon a little of the mixture onto each of the greaseproof paper squares, then place the fish on top. Divide the remaining tomato mixture among the fish.

4 Fold up the paper around the fish, twisting it into tiny pleats to seal securely. Place the parcels on a baking sheet and bake in a preheated oven, 200°C/400°F/ Gas Mark 6, for 15 minutes.

5 Transfer the parcels to warmed plates and cut off the folded edges of the parcels. Serve with bread.

variations
Red snapper can be used rather than red mullet. Substitute chopped fresh fennel leaves for the rosemary and add 2–3 parboiled new potatoes to the parcels.

introduced after the *secondo*, as a palate cleanser and a 'breathing space'. They may also be served as an accompaniment to a meat or fish dish. Simple green salads often appear on the menu, but usually include a greater variety of leaves than just lettuce: chicory, radicchio, rocket, baby spinach and fresh herbs may all feature. However, salads are also made with a vast range of vegetables and other ingredients, including peppers, mushrooms, tomatoes, cheese, anchovies, onions, oranges, capers and olives, although only a few, complementary flavours are combined in any one dish. A classic example of this is *Insalata Tricolore* (see page 220), a perfect mix of mozzarella cheese, sliced tomatoes and fresh basil leaves.

Salads are usually dressed with a simple vinaigrette made with olive oil and vinegar or freshly squeezed

Italians treat their vegetables with respect, almost reverence, rather than as an afterthought to accompany a main dish

lemon juice. For the best results, select an extra virgin olive oil, which has the fullest and fruitiest flavour. An interesting variation is to use walnut oil, which used to be far less expensive than olive oil because walnut trees grew all over Lombardy and other parts of northern Italy. The walnut flavour goes well with robust, peasant-style salads, although sadly it is now an expensive oil, in Italy and elsewhere.

parmesan pumpkin
zucca alla parmigiana

Pumpkin is a popular vegetable in some countries – including all regions of Italy – and virtually ignored in others. This rich dish will instantly convert those who have never tried it.

SERVES 6

2 tbsp virgin olive oil

1 onion, chopped finely

1 garlic clove, chopped finely

400 ml/14 fl oz passata

10 fresh basil leaves, shredded

2 tbsp chopped fresh flat-leaved parsley

1 tsp sugar

salt and pepper

2 eggs, beaten lightly

55 g/2 oz dried, uncoloured breadcrumbs

1.6 kg/3½ lb pumpkin, peeled, deseeded and sliced

55 g/2 oz butter, plus extra for greasing

55 g/2 oz freshly grated Parmesan cheese

1 Heat the olive oil in a large saucepan, add the onion and garlic and cook over a low heat for 5 minutes, until softened. Stir in the passata, basil, parsley and sugar and season to taste with salt and pepper. Simmer for 10-15 minutes, until thickened.

2 Meanwhile, put the beaten eggs in a shallow dish and spread out the breadcrumbs in another shallow dish. Dip the slices of pumpkin first in the egg, then in the breadcrumbs to coat, shaking off any excess.

3 Grease a large ovenproof dish with butter. Melt the butter in a large, heavy-based frying pan. Add the pumpkin slices, in batches, and cook until browned all over. Transfer the slices to the dish. Pour the sauce over them and sprinkle with the Parmesan.

4 Bake in a preheated oven 180°C/350°F/Gas Mark 4, for 30 minutes, until the cheese is bubbling and golden. Serve immediately.

The skyline of Florence seems a view from a bygone age

202

sweet and sour onions
cipolline in agrodolce

SERVES 4

55 g/2 oz unsalted butter

5 tbsp white granulated sugar

2 tbsp balsamic vinegar

125 ml/4 fl oz white wine vinegar

650 g/1 lb 7 oz button onions

salt and pepper

This combination of sweet and sour is a favourite Italian way of cooking all kinds of foods, from vegetables, such as courgettes and globe artichokes, to game, such as rabbit and hare. You can serve these onions as an accompaniment to roasts and grills or as part of an antipasti.

1 Melt the butter in a heavy-based frying pan over a low heat. Add the sugar and heat, stirring constantly, until it has dissolved.

2 Stir in the balsamic and white wine vinegars, then add the onions and season to taste with salt and pepper.

3 Increase the heat to medium, cover and cook for 25 minutes, until the onions are tender and golden. Serve immediately.

braised courgettes
zucchini alla calabrese

This quick and easy accompaniment goes superbly well with grilled meat or fish.

SERVES 4

2 tbsp olive oil

2 red onions, chopped

1 garlic clove, chopped finely

5 courgettes, cut into 1–cm/¹/₂–inch thick slices

150 ml/¹/₄ pint vegetable stock

1 tsp chopped fresh oregano

salt and pepper

1 Heat the olive oil in a large, heavy-based frying pan. Add the onions and garlic and cook over a medium heat, stirring occasionally, for 5 minutes until softened and beginning to colour.

2 Add the courgettes and cook, stirring frequently, for 4–5 minutes, until just beginning to colour.

3 Pour in the stock, add the oregano and season to taste with salt and pepper. Lower the heat and simmer gently for about 10 minutes, until all the liquid has evaporated. Serve immediately.

variation
Add 200 g/7 oz diced pancetta or rindless streaky bacon with the onions in step 1.

204 # braised fennel
finocchi stufati

Slow braising is a traditional Italian way of cooking many vegetables, as it intensifies the flavour, but also makes it more subtle.

SERVES 4

2 fennel bulbs

1 tbsp olive oil

1 onion, sliced thinly

2 tomatoes, peeled (see page 36) and chopped

55 g/2 oz black olives, stoned

150 ml/¼ pint vegetable stock

2 tbsp torn fresh basil leaves

pepper

1 Cut off and chop the fennel fronds and reserve for garnishing. Cut the bulbs in half lengthways, then slice them thinly.

2 Heat the olive oil in a heavy-based frying pan. Add the onion and cook over a low heat, stirring occasionally, for 5 minutes, until softened. Add the fennel slices and cook, stirring occasionally, for a further 10 minutes.

3 Add the tomatoes and olives and pour in enough stock to cover the base of the frying pan. Cover and simmer gently for 20 minutes, until the fennel is very tender. Stir in the basil and season to taste with pepper. Transfer to a warmed serving dish, garnish with the reserved fennel fronds and serve immediately.

variation

If you prefer your fennel crisper, omit the stock in step 3 and cook the fennel mixture over a medium heat, stirring frequently, for about 10 minutes, before adding the basil and seasoning.

stewed peppers, tomatoes and onions
peperonata

Just about every region of Italy has its own favourite pepper speciality, but this must be the best-known and most popular recipe.

SERVES 4

5 tbsp olive oil

2 large onions, sliced thinly

1 garlic clove, chopped finely

3 red peppers, deseeded and cut into strips

3 yellow peppers, deseeded and cut into strips

12 tomatoes, peeled (see page 36) and chopped

salt

1 tbsp white wine vinegar

variation

For *Peperonata alla Romana*, stir in 1 tablespoon rinsed capers just before serving.

1 Heat the olive oil in a heavy-based frying pan. Add the onions, garlic and peppers and cook over a low heat, stirring occasionally, for 15 minutes.

2 Add the tomatoes and season to taste with salt. Stir in the vinegar, cover and simmer for 30 minutes, until very tender. Serve immediately.

206

peppers and potatoes
peperoni e patate

In Italy, potatoes are often combined with other vegetables, rather than cooked as a separate accompaniment. Here, mixed peppers provide plenty of colour and extra flavour, while fresh chilli gives additional bite.

SERVES 4

1 fresh red chilli, deseeded

2 garlic cloves

bunch of fresh flat-leaved parsley

125 ml/4 fl oz virgin olive oil

450 g/1 lb waxy potatoes, sliced thinly

2 tbsp hot water (optional)

450 g/1 lb mixed red and orange peppers,
  deseeded and diced

salt

1 Place the chilli, garlic and parsley on a chopping board and chop together until very fine and well mixed. Heat half the oil in a large, heavy-based frying pan. Add half the chilli mixture and cook over a medium heat, stirring constantly, for 1 minute.

2 Add the potatoes, lower the heat and cook, turning frequently, for 15-20 minutes. Add the hot water if the potato slices begin to stick.

3 Meanwhile, heat the remaining oil in another frying pan, add the remaining chilli mixture and cook over a medium heat, stirring constantly, for 1 minute. Add the peppers and cook, stirring frequently, for 15-20 minutes, until tender.

4 Combine the potato and pepper mixtures in a large warmed serving bowl, season with salt and serve immediately.

*cook's tip
If the potatoes are tender before the peppers are cooked, cover the saucepan with a lid to keep them warm.

Winding streets of a typical traditional Tuscan village

Overleaf *The dome of St Peter's Church as dusk falls over Rome*

210

spinach and ricotta dumplings
gnocchi di spinaci e ricotta

These mouthwatering dumplings, made with spinach and ricotta cheese are best served simply, coated in a herb butter and sprinkled with Parmesan cheese.

SERVES 4

1 kg/2 lb 4 oz fresh spinach, tough stalks removed

350 g/12 oz ricotta cheese

115 g/4 oz freshly grated Parmesan cheese

3 eggs, beaten lightly

pinch of freshly grated nutmeg

salt and pepper

115–175 g/4–6 oz plain flour, plus extra for dusting

for the herb butter

115 g/4 oz unsalted butter

2 tbsp chopped fresh oregano

2 tbsp chopped fresh sage

1 Wash the spinach, then place it in a saucepan with just the water clinging to its leaves. Cover and cook over a low heat for 6–8 minutes, until just wilted. Drain well and set aside to cool.

2 Squeeze or press out as much liquid as possible from the spinach*, then chop finely or process in a food processor or blender. Place the spinach in a bowl and add the ricotta, half the Parmesan, the eggs and nutmeg and season to taste with salt and pepper. Beat until thoroughly combined. Begin by sifting in 115 g/4 oz of the flour and lightly work it into the mixture, adding more, if necessary, to make a workable mixture. Cover with clingfilm and chill for 1 hour.

3 With floured hands, break off small pieces of the mixture and roll them into walnut-sized balls. Handle them as little as possible, as they are quite delicate. Lightly dust the dumplings with flour.

4 Bring a large saucepan of lightly salted water to the boil. Add the dumplings and cook for 2–3 minutes, until they rise to the surface. Remove them from the saucepan with a slotted spoon, drain well and set aside.

5 Meanwhile, make the herb butter. Melt the butter in a large, heavy-based frying pan. Add the oregano and sage and cook over a low heat, stirring frequently, for 1 minute. Add the dumplings and toss gently for 1 minute to coat. Transfer to a warmed serving dish, sprinkle with the remaining Parmesan and serve.

*cook's tip
A good way to remove the liquid from cooked spinach is to put it in a sieve and use a potato masher to press out the unwanted water.

basil dumplings
gnocchi alla genovese

In Italy, gnocchi are traditionally served as a primo or first course, but they can also make an unusual and delicious accompaniment to meat or fish.

700 ml/1¼ pints milk

200 g/7 oz semolina

1 tbsp finely chopped fresh basil leaves

4 sun-dried tomatoes in oil, drained and chopped finely

2 eggs, beaten lightly

55 g/2 oz butter, plus extra for greasing

85 g/3 oz freshly grated Parmesan cheese

salt and pepper

Tomato Sauce (see page 106), to serve

1 Pour the milk into a large saucepan and bring to just below boiling point. Sprinkle in the semolina, stirring constantly. Lower the heat and simmer gently for about 2 minutes, until thick and smooth. Remove the saucepan from the heat.

2 Stir in the basil, sun-dried tomatoes, eggs, half the butter and half the Parmesan and season to taste with salt and pepper. Stir well until all the ingredients are thoroughly incorporated, then pour into a shallow dish or baking tray and level the surface. Set aside to cool, then chill for at least 1 hour, until set.

3 Lightly grease an ovenproof dish with butter. Using a lightly floured, plain, round cutter, stamp out rounds of the set semolina mixture. Place the trimmings in the base of the dish and top with the rounds.

4 Melt the remaining butter and brush it over the semolina rounds, then sprinkle with the remaining Parmesan. Bake in a preheated oven, 190°C/375°F/Gas Mark 5, for 30-35 minutes, until golden. Serve immediately with tomato sauce.

porcini mushroom salad 215
insalata di funghi porcini

1 Thinly slice 450 g/1 lb of the mushrooms and arrange them on a serving platter. Finely chop the remaining mushrooms and set aside (depending on their size there may be only one or even only part of one remaining).

2 Put the olive oil and garlic in a heavy-based frying pan and heat gently for 1 minute. Remove the garlic with a slotted spoon and discard.

3 Add the chopped mushrooms, season with salt, cover and cook over a low heat for 3–4 minutes. Remove the frying pan from the heat and cool slightly.

4 Transfer the warm mushroom mixture to a food processor or blender and process until smooth. Return the mixture to the frying pan.

5 Set the frying pan over a low heat and gradually beat in the butter, a piece at a time, until it is fully incorporated. Do not allow the mixture to boil.

6 Meanwhile, place the platter of sliced mushrooms in a preheated oven, 120°C/250°F/Gas Mark ½, to warm through slightly.

7 Stir the parsley into the sauce, pour it over the mushrooms and serve warm.

variation
For a less indulgent dish, substitute other wild mushrooms for the porcini.

This is the most gloriously extravagant salad, but worth every euro. Of course, housekeeping budgets are helped by the fact that Italians are keen gatherers of wild mushrooms.

SERVES 4
500 g/1 lb 2 oz fresh porcini mushrooms
1 tbsp extra virgin olive oil
1 garlic clove
salt
200 g/7 oz unsalted butter, diced
1 tbsp chopped fresh flat-leaved parsley

216 # mozzarella salad with sun-dried tomatoes
mozzarella alla romana

Mozzarella is often included in salads, but this recipe from Rome is a more sophisticated version, as befits Italy's capital city.

SERVES 4

140 g/5 oz sun-dried tomatoes in olive oil
  (drained weight), reserving the oil from the bottle

15 g/^{1}/$_2$ oz fresh basil, shredded coarsely

15 g/^{1}/$_2$ oz fresh flat-leaved parsley, chopped coarsely

1 tbsp capers, rinsed

1 tbsp balsamic vinegar

1 garlic clove, chopped coarsely

extra olive oil, if necessary

pepper

100 g/3^1/$_2$ oz mixed salad leaves, such as oakleaf
  lettuce, baby spinach and rocket

500 g/1 lb 2 oz smoked mozzarella, sliced

1 Put the sun-dried tomatoes, basil, parsley, capers, vinegar and garlic in a food processor or blender. Measure the oil from the sun-dried tomatoes jar and make it up to 150 ml/^{1}/$_4$ pint with more olive oil if necessary. Add it to the food processor or blender and process until smooth. Season to taste with pepper.

2 Divide the salad leaves among 4 individual serving plates. Top with the slices of mozzarella and spoon the dressing over them. Serve immediately.

variation
Substitute taleggio or a goat's milk cheese for the mozzarella.

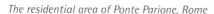

The residential area of Ponte Parione, Rome

layered tomato salad
la panzanella

This is a popular salad throughout Italy and the perfect way of using up yesterday's bread. For the fullest flavour, use sun-ripened tomatoes.

SERVES 4

1 red onion, sliced thinly into rings

4 slices day-old bread

450 g/1 lb tomatoes, sliced thinly

115 g/4 oz mozzarella di bufala, sliced thinly

1 tbsp shredded fresh basil

salt and pepper

125 ml/4 fl oz extra virgin olive oil

3 tbsp balsamic vinegar

4 tbsp lemon juice

115 g/4 oz black olives, stoned and sliced thinly

1 Place the onion slices in a bowl and add cold water to cover. Set aside to soak for 10 minutes. Meanwhile, dip the slices of bread in a shallow dish of cold water, then squeeze out the excess. Place the bread in a serving dish.

2 Drain the onion slices and layer them on the bread with the tomatoes and mozzarella, sprinkling each layer with the basil and salt and pepper.

3 Pour over the olive oil, vinegar and lemon juice and sprinkle with the sliced olive. Cover and chill for up to 8 hours before serving.

Typical hilltop Tuscan village

artichoke and rocket salad 223
insalata di carciofi e rucola

This simple Tuscan salad is made from the small, tender artichokes of the early summer, but can also be made from the closely related cardoon. If using cardoons, cut off and discard the tough, outer stalks.

SERVES 4

8 baby globe artichokes

juice of 2 lemons

bunch of rocket

salt and pepper

125 ml/4 fl oz extra virgin olive oil

115 g/4 oz pecorino cheese

1 Break off the stems of the artichokes and cut off about 2.5 cm/1 inch of the tops, depending on how young and small they are. Remove and discard any coarse outer leaves, leaving only the pale, tender inner leaves. Using a teaspoon scoop out the chokes. Rub each artichoke with lemon juice as soon as it is prepared to prevent it from discolouring.

2 Thinly slice the artichokes and place in a salad bowl. Add the rocket, lemon juice and olive oil, season to taste with salt and pepper and toss well.

3 Using a swivel-blade vegetable peeler, thinly shave the pecorino over the salad, then serve immediately.

variation
If only larger artichokes are available, cook them in lightly salted boiling water for about 15 minutes, then refresh under cold running water before slicing.

Palace façade on the edge of Lake Como

224 # pasta salad with chargrilled peppers
insalata di peperoni arrostiti

Traditionalists eat their pasta before the main course, and they eat it hot. Nevertheless, the booming tourist industry has brought some compromises in its wake – if only for those not fortunate enough to have been born in Italy.

SERVES 4

1 red pepper

1 orange pepper

280 g/10 oz dried conchiglie

5 tbsp extra virgin olive oil

2 tbsp lemon juice

2 tbsp Pesto (see page 36)

1 garlic clove

3 tbsp shredded fresh basil leaves

salt and pepper

1 Put the whole peppers on a baking sheet and place under a preheated grill, turning frequently, for 15 minutes, until charred all over. Remove with tongs and place in a bowl. Cover with crumpled kitchen paper and set aside.

2 Meanwhile, bring a large saucepan of lightly salted water to the boil. Add the pasta, bring back to the boil and cook for 8–10 minutes, until tender, but still firm to the bite.

3 Combine the olive oil, lemon juice, pesto and garlic in a bowl, whisking well to mix. Drain the pasta, add it to the pesto mixture while still hot and toss well. Set aside.

4 When the peppers are cool enough to handle, peel off the skins, then cut open and remove the seeds. Chop the flesh coarsely and add to the pasta with the basil. Season to taste with salt and pepper and toss well. Serve at room temperature.

variation

A more traditional salad, without the pasta, can be made in the same way. When the peppers have been under the grill for 10 minutes, add 4 tomatoes and grill for a further 5 minutes. Cover the peppers with kitchen paper, then peel and chop as in step 4. Peel and coarsely chop the tomatoes. Combine them with the dressing and garnish with black olives.

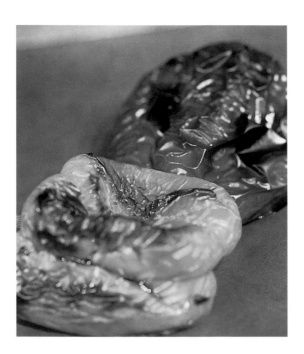

DESSERTS, CAKES & DRINKS

Go to Rome for ice creams, to Florence for zabaglione and to anywhere in the south of Italy for cheesecake and sticky, honey-flavoured desserts. Italians don't prepare and cook desserts at home as a general rule, but if they want to celebrate a special occasion, they will do so in style. Finally, top and tail your meal with a delicious cocktail to start and superb coffee to end.

Everyday meals in Italy usually conclude with fresh fruit, possibly a choice of cheese, but on special occasions desserts are served. These are often elaborate confections bought from the local *pasticceria*, or mouthwatering ice creams from the *gelateria*. One ice cream parlour in Rome claims to be the best in the world and boasts over 200 different flavours.

However, there are Italian desserts within the scope of the home cook, which are still luxurious enough to be considered a special treat. *Tiramisù* (see page 238), a rich mixture of mascarpone cheese, coffee liqueur, chocolate and biscuits, has conquered half the world since its invention in the 1970s, not least because it is so easy to make. Making ice cream at home is time-consuming, but a *Semifreddo* (see page 250), or a *Granita* (see page 251), require very little effort for surprisingly impressive results. Some of the traditional desserts do demand a little more skill and practice. The deceptively simple *Zabaglione* (see page 239), for instance, must be beaten to precisely the right degree of creamy thickness for just the right length of time and then served immediately.

Many of the most delicious desserts come from southern Italy and from Sicily and Sardinia. This has much to do with the ample fruit, nuts and honey produced in these parts. *Cassata alla Siciliana* (see page 248), for example, is a sponge cake filled with a lavish blend of ricotta cheese, cherry liqueur, candied fruits and chocolate, covered with double cream.

Home baking is not a major activity in the Italian kitchen because there are bakers and confectioners in every town and village. Most special baking is left to these professionals, but some cooks are happy to make the occasional cheesecake or chocolate loaf – a cross between a tea bread and a cake. However, there is no reason why keen cooks should not try their hand at baking a more specialist recipe such as *panforte*, the traditional Christmas cake from the Tuscan city of Sienna.

Italy is the world's largest wine producer, so it is hardly surprising that wine is drunk with most meals. There are several brands of Italian beer and a number of popular apéritifs for pre-dinner drinks, as well as a selection of liqueurs to accompany an after-dinner *espresso*. While there is no 'national drink' in the way that Spain boasts its *sangría*, there are a number of internationally famous cocktails based on Italian ingredients. Italian vermouth features in numerous mixed drinks, even though the Dry Martini was not named after the famous brand, but after its inventor, Martini de Anna de Toggia. The lovely crimson colour of Campari, first manufactured by the Campari brothers in Milan in the 19th century, makes it a natural choice for cocktails, among them the elegant

One ice cream parlour in Rome claims to be the best in the world and boasts over 200 different flavours

Negroni (see page 253), the popular Americano and the more unusual Italian Stallion. Another Lombardy liqueur, the bright yellow, herb-flavoured Galliano, features in a number of contemporary cocktails, including the Harvey Wallbanger. Amaretto, made from apricot kernels and with a distinctive almond flavour, is also a favourite for mixed drinks, including an entire family of Godfather, Godmother and several other relatives. Perhaps the most delicious and

Italian grapes make wines with a very distinctive character. These bunches are drying on racks to concentrate the fruit

Overleaf *Elegant detailing on window frames and ironwork are typical of many fine Italian buildings*

least controversial way to serve it, apart from as a straightforward liqueur, is to make the Italian equivalent to Irish coffee, *Espresso Amaretto* (see page 252).

236 # mascarpone creams
crema di mascarpone

Rich and self-indulgent, these creamy desserts make the perfect end to a special occasion meal.

SERVES 4
115 g/4 oz amaretti, crushed

4 tbsp Amaretto or Maraschino

4 eggs, separated

55 g/2 oz caster sugar

225 g/8 oz mascarpone cheese

toasted flaked almonds, to decorate

1 Place the amaretti crumbs in a bowl, add the Amaretto or Maraschino and set aside to soak.

2 Meanwhile, beat the egg yolks with the caster sugar until pale and thick. Fold in the mascarpone and soaked biscuit crumbs.

3 Whisk the egg white in a separate, spotlessly clean, bowl until stiff, then gently fold into the cheese mixture. Divide the mascarpone cream among 4 serving dishes and chill for 1-2 hours. Sprinkle with flaked almonds just before serving.

*cook's tip
The easiest way to make biscuit crumbs is to place the biscuits in a plastic bag and crush with a rolling pin.

238
creamy coffee and chocolate dessert
tiramisù

This rich and popular dessert is a relatively new invention, dating from the 1970s, but it quickly acquired global appeal. The name means 'pick me up', but it isn't clear whether this is because it is so delicious that it acts as a tonic or so wonderful that you faint with delight on tasting it and have to be picked up off the floor!

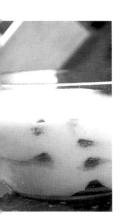

SERVES 6

2 eggs, separated, plus 2 egg yolks

100 g/3¹/₂ oz caster sugar

1 tsp vanilla essence

500 g/1 lb 2 oz mascarpone cheese

175 ml/6 fl oz strong black coffee

125 ml/4 fl oz Kahlúa, Tía Maria, rum or brandy

24 boudoir or sponge fingers

2 tbsp cocoa powder

2 tbsp finely grated plain chocolate

1 Whisk the 4 egg yolks with the sugar and vanilla essence in the top of a double saucepan or in a heatproof bowl set over a saucepan of barely simmering water. When the mixture is pale and so thick that the whisk leaves a ribbon trail when lifted, remove the bowl from the heat and set aside to cool completely. Whisk the mixture occasionally to prevent a skin from forming.

2 When the egg yolk mixture is quite cool, whisk the mascarpone into the egg yolk mixture until thoroughly combined. With clean blades, whisk the egg whites in a separate, spotlessly clean, bowl until they form soft peaks, then gently fold them into the mascarpone mixture with a figure-of-eight action.

3 Combine the coffee and liqueur, rum or brandy in a shallow dish. Dip the boudoir or sponge fingers into the mixture, one at a time, turning them quickly so that they absorb the liquid but do not fall apart. Arrange a layer of biscuits on the base of a serving dish.

4 Spoon about one-third of the mascarpone mixture on top, spreading it out evenly. Repeat the layers, dipping and turning the biscuits quickly in the coffee mixture. Finish with a layer of the mascarpone mixture and smooth the surface. Chill for at least 1 hour or, preferably, overnight before serving.

5 Just before serving, sift the cocoa powder evenly over the top of the dessert, then sprinkle with the grated chocolate.

foaming froth
zabaglione

*This world-famous dessert gets its name from a
Neapolitan dialect word,* zapillare, *which means to
foam and that sums up exactly the texture required.
It is quite difficult to achieve the right texture of the
egg yolks without their curdling, but it is certainly
worth the effort.*

SERVES 4
4 egg yolks
60 g/2¼ oz caster sugar
5 tbsp Marsala
amaretti biscuits, to serve

1 Whisk the egg yolks with the sugar in a heatproof
bowl or, if you have one, the top of a double
saucepan for about 1 minute.

2 Gently whisk in the Marsala. Set the bowl over
a saucepan of barely simmering water or put the
top of the double saucepan on its base filled with
barely simmering water, and whisk vigorously for
10–15 minutes, until thick, creamy and foamy.

3 Immediately pour into serving glasses and serve
with amaretti.

variations
You can use other wines, such as Champagne, Sauternes
or Madeira to flavour this dessert, or a liqueur, such as
Chartreuse or Cointreau. You could also use a mixture
of white wine and brandy, rum or Maraschino.

almond cake
torta di mandorle

This rich cake is delicious served with fruit as a dessert or simply with a cup of coffee for a mid-morning snack. Using potato flour is the secret of its wonderful, soft texture.

MAKES 1 x 20-cm/8-inch CAKE

butter, for greasing

3 eggs, separated

140 g/ 5 oz caster sugar

55 g/2 oz potato flour

140 g/5 oz almonds, blanched, peeled and chopped finely

finely grated rind of 1 orange

135 ml/4¹/₄ fl oz orange juice

salt

icing sugar, for dusting

1 Generously grease a round 20-cm/8-inch cake tin. Beat the egg yolks with the sugar in a medium bowl until pale and thick and the mixture leaves a ribbon trail when the whisk is lifted. Stir in the potato flour, almonds, orange rind and orange juice.

2 Whisk the egg whites with a pinch of salt in another bowl until stiff. Gently fold the whites into the egg yolk mixture.

3 Pour the mixture into the tin and bake in a preheated oven, 160°C/325°F/Gas Mark 3, for 50-60 minutes, until golden and just firm to the touch. Turn out on to a wire rack to cool. Sift over a little icing sugar to decorate before serving.

A typical Venetian backwater

242

tuscan christmas cake
panforte di siena

No celebration of Italian cooking can ignore this famous spicy Christmas cake*. It is extremely rich: keep your portions small.

SERVES 12–14

115 g/4 oz hazelnuts

115 g/4 oz almonds

85 g/3 oz candied peel

55 g/2 oz ready-to-eat dried apricots, chopped finely

55 g/2 oz candied pineapple, chopped finely

grated rind of 1 orange

55 g/2 oz plain flour

2 tbsp cocoa powder

1 tsp ground cinnamon

1/4 tsp ground coriander

1/4 tsp freshly grated nutmeg

1/4 tsp ground cloves

115 g/4 oz caster sugar

175 g/6 oz clear honey

icing sugar, to decorate

equipment

20-cm/8-inch loose-based cake tin

1 Line the cake tin with baking paper. Spread out the hazelnuts on a baking sheet and toast in a preheated oven, 180°C/350°F/Gas Mark 4, for 10 minutes, until golden brown. Tip them on to a tea towel and rub off the skins. Meanwhile, spread out the almonds on a baking sheet and toast in the oven for 10 minutes, until golden. Watch carefully after 7 minutes as they can burn easily. Lower the oven temperature to 150°C/300°F/Gas Mark 2. Chop all the nuts and place in a large bowl.

2 Add the candied peel, apricots, pineapple and orange rind to the nuts and mix well. Sift together the flour, cocoa powder, cinnamon, coriander, nutmeg and cloves into the bowl and mix well.

3 Put the sugar and honey into a saucepan and set over a low heat, stirring, until the sugar has dissolved. Bring to the boil and cook for 5 minutes, until thickened and beginning to darken. Stir the nut mixture into the saucepan and remove from the heat.

4 Spoon the mixture into the prepared cake tin and smooth the surface with the back of a damp spoon. Bake in the oven for 1 hour, then transfer to a wire rack to cool in the tin.

5 Carefully remove the cake from the tin and peel off the baking paper. Just before serving, dredge the top with icing sugar. Cut into thin wedges to serve.

*cook's tip
You can make this cake up to 2 weeks in advance. Store in an airtight container.

Overleaf *The main cathedral, Milan*

246

stuffed peaches
pesche ripiene alla piemontese

Peaches grow throughout central and southern Italy – in fact this recipe comes from the Piedmont in the northwest.

SERVES 6

55 g/2 oz unsalted butter, plus extra for greasing

6 large peaches*

25 g/1 oz ground almonds

55 g/2 oz amaretti biscuits, crushed coarsely

1 tbsp Amaretto liqueur

$^{1}/_{2}$ tsp grated lemon rind

1 tsp cocoa powder

2 tsp icing sugar

225 ml/8 fl oz medium–dry white wine

1 Grease an ovenproof dish with butter. Cut the peaches in half, remove and discard the stones. Widen the central cavity by cutting away and reserving some of the flesh in a bowl.

2 Add the almonds, amaretti, Amaretto, lemon rind and half the butter to the reserved peach flesh and mash with a fork. Fill the peach cavities with this mixture and place them in the dish.

3 Dot the peaches with the remaining butter and sprinkle with the cocoa powder and icing sugar. Pour the wine into the dish and bake in a preheated oven, 180°C/350°F/Gas Mark 4, for 30 minutes, until golden. Serve immediately.

cook's tip
Use white peaches if you can find them, as they have the sweetest and most succulent flavour. White or yellow, do make sure the peaches are really ripe.

marsala cherries
ciliege al marsala

This is a popular Venetian dish, made with Morello cherries – the variety most widely grown in Italy.

SERVES 4

140 g/5 oz caster sugar

thinly pared rind of 1 lemon

5-cm/2-inch piece of cinnamon stick

225 ml/8 fl oz water

225 ml/8 fl oz Marsala

900 g/2 lb Morello cherries, stoned

150 ml/¼ pint double cream

1 Put the sugar, lemon rind, cinnamon stick, water and Marsala in a heavy-based saucepan and bring to the boil, stirring constantly. Lower the heat and simmer for 5 minutes. Remove the cinnamon stick.

2 Add the Morello cherries, cover and simmer gently for 10 minutes. Using a slotted spoon, transfer the cherries to a bowl.

3 Return the saucepan to the heat and bring to the boil over a high heat. Boil for 3–4 minutes, until thick and syrupy. Pour the syrup over the cherries and set aside to cool, then chill for at least 1 hour.

4 Whisk the cream until stiff peaks form. Divide the cherries and syrup among 4 individual dishes or glasses, top with the cream and serve.

variation
Substitute a full-bodied red wine for the Marsala.

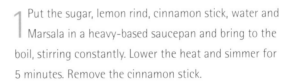

248

sicilian ice cream cake
cassata alla siciliana

Nowhere in Italy do they produce such lavish desserts as in Sicily. While the term cassata, *which means 'brick' and refers to the shape of the dessert, is usually applied to a luxurious ice cream, this glorious confection is an elaborate cake.*

SERVES 4

for the Genoa sponge cake

6 eggs, separated

200 g/7 oz caster sugar

85 g/3 oz self-raising flour

85 g/3 oz cornflour

for the filling

500 g/1 lb 2 oz ricotta cheese

200 g/7 oz caster sugar

600 ml/1 pint Maraschino* liqueur

85 g/3 oz plain chocolate

200 g/7 oz mixed candied peel, diced

300 ml/¹/₂ pint double cream

to decorate

glacé cherries, angelica, candied fruit and slivered almonds

equipment

25-cm/10-inch springform cake tin

900-g/2-lb loaf tin

1 First, line the cake tin with baking paper for the sponge cake.

2 Beat the egg yolks with the sugar until pale and frothy. In a separate, spotlessly clean, bowl, whisk the whites until stiff peaks form. Gently fold the whites into the egg yolk mixture with a figure-of-eight action.

3 Sift together the flour and cornflour into a bowl, then sift into the egg mixture and gently fold in. Pour the mixture into the cake tin and smooth the surface. Bake in a preheated oven, 180°C/350°F/Gas Mark 4, for 30 minutes, until springy to the touch of a fingertip. Turn out onto a wire rack, remove the lining paper and set aside to cool completely.

4 For the filling, combine the ricotta, sugar and 400 ml/14 fl oz of the Maraschino in a bowl, beating well. Chop the chocolate with a knife and stir it into the mixture with the candied fruit.

5 Cut the sponge cake into strips about 1 cm/¹/₂ inch wide and use it to line the base and sides of the loaf tin. Set aside the remaining slices.

6 Spoon the ricotta mixture into the tin and smooth the surface. Cover the filling with the reserved strips of sponge cake. Drizzle the remaining Maraschino over the top, then chill overnight.

7 Run a round-bladed knife around the sides of the tin and turn out onto a serving plate. Whisk the double cream until stiff peaks form. Coat the top and sides of the cake with the cream and decorate with the cherries, angelica, candied fruit and almonds.

*cook's tip

Maraschino is a sweet, colourless liqueur made from fermented bitter Maraschino cherries. If you prefer, you can use Cointreau.

chilled chocolate dessert
semifreddo al cioccolato

The range of Italian ice creams, sorbets and water ices is breathtaking. This melt-in-the-mouth speciality is 'semi-frozen' – a cross between a mousse and an ice cream.

SERVES 4-6

225 g/8 oz mascarpone cheese
2 tbsp finely ground coffee beans
25 g/1 oz icing sugar
85 g/3 oz plain chocolate, grated finely
350 ml/12 fl oz double cream, plus extra to decorate
Marsala, to serve

1 Beat the mascarpone with the coffee and icing sugar until thoroughly combined.

2 Set aside 4 teaspoons of the grated chocolate and stir the remainder into the cheese mixture with 5 tablespoons of the unwhipped cream.

3 Whisk the remaining cream until it forms soft peaks. Stir 1 tablespoon of the mascarpone mixture into the cream to slacken it, then fold the cream into the remaining mascarpone mixture with a figure-of-eight action.

4 Spoon the mixture into a freezerproof container and place in the freezer for about 3 hours.*

5 To serve, scoop the chocolate dessert into sundae glasses and drizzle with a little Marsala. Top with whipped cream and decorate with the reserved grated chocolate. Serve immediately.

*cook's tip
Do not freeze the mixture for too long or it will lose its texture.

Halfway between a cold drink and a sorbet, a refreshing granita with a citrus tang is the perfect midsummer dessert. Alternatively, you can serve it between courses as a palate cleanser.

SERVES 4
450 ml/16 fl oz water
115 g/4 oz white granulated sugar
225 ml/8 fl oz lemon juice
grated rind of 1 lemon

lemon granita
granita al limone

1 Heat the water in a heavy-based saucepan over a low heat. Add the sugar and stir until it has completely dissolved. Bring to the boil, remove the saucepan from the heat and set the syrup aside to cool.

2 Stir the lemon juice and rind into the syrup. Pour the mixture into a freezerproof container and place in the freezer for 3–4 hours.

3 To serve, remove the container from the freezer and dip the base into hot water. Turn out the ice block and chop coarsely, then place in a food processor* and process until it forms small crystals (*granita* means 'granular'). Spoon into sundae glasses and serve immediately.

variations
Many different fruit syrups can be used to flavour granitas – oranges, mandarins, pink grapefruit or mangoes. Simply substitute the juice in step 2. You can add extra flavour with a splash of liqueur or include herbs, such as lemon balm, or elderflower in the syrup in step 1 (strain before pouring into the freezer container). Coffee granita made with espresso coffee instead of fruit juice, with or without a dash of liqueur, is also delicious.

*cook's tip
An ordinary blender may not be sufficiently robust to process the ice as it can damage the blades. A good-quality food processor is recommended.

252

amaretto coffee
espresso amaretto

This is a lovely variation of Irish coffee. Amaretto is a deliciously sweet, almond-flavoured liqueur made from apricot kernels. It is delicious drunk on its own, but it also forms the basis of a number of cocktails (see variations).

SERVES 1

30 ml/1 fl oz Amaretto

1 cup hot black coffee

1 tbsp double cream

1 Pour the Amaretto into the cup of coffee and stir so the flavour mixes in well with the coffee.

2 Hold a teaspoon, rounded side upward, against the side of the cup with the tip just touching the surface of the coffee. Pour the cream over the back of the spoon so that it floats on top of the coffee. Serve immediately.

variations

For a Godfather, put 50 ml/2 fl oz Scotch whisky and 30 ml/1 fl oz Amaretto into a chilled glass filled with ice cubes. Stir well and serve. For an Amaretto Rose, pour 30 ml/1 fl oz Amaretto and 1 teaspoon lime cordial into a chilled glass filled with ice cubes. Stir well and top up with soda water or sparkling mineral water.

negroni
negroni

This aristocratic cocktail was invented by Count Negroni at the Bar Giacosa in Florence. Its colour derives from Campari, the beautifully crimson aperitivo with a bitter flavour, named after the brothers who first produced it in the nineteenth century and still made by the same family. Campari is often drunk simply with soda, but there are a number of other classic Campari cocktails (see variations).

SERVES 1
ice cubes
30 ml/1 fl oz Campari
30 ml/1 fl oz dry gin
30 ml/1 fl oz Italian sweet vermouth

1 Put the ice cubes into a jug. Pour in the Campari, gin and vermouth and stir well.

2 Strain off the ice cubes into a cocktail glass and serve immediately.

variations

To make an Americano, put some ice cubes into a jug and pour in 30 ml/1 fl oz Campari and 30 ml/1 fl oz Italian sweet vermouth. Stir to mix, then strain into a tall glass. Top up with soda or sparkling mineral water and decorate with a slice of orange. To make an After One, put some ice cubes into a jug and pour in 30 ml/1 fl oz Campari, 30 ml/1 fl oz dry gin, 30 ml/1 fl oz Italian sweet vermouth and 30 ml/1 fl oz Galliano. Stir to mix and strain into a cocktail glass.

index